Ελα Μαζί Μου
(Ela Mazí Mou)

Come With Me:
A Memoir of a Cypriot Girl's Resilient Life Journey

Stories told by Roula Santamas
Transcribed, written, and narrated
by Irene Santamas-Kulbacki

NFB
Buffalo, New York

Printed in the United States of America

Come With Me: A Memoir of a Cypriot Girl's Resilient Life Journey/
Santamas-Kulbacki 1st Edition

ISBN: 978-1-953610-66-9

Nonfiction> Memoir
Nonfiction> Biography
Nonfiction> Family Dynamic
Nonfiction> Cypriot Heritage

NFB Publishing
119 Dorchester Road
Buffalo, New York 14213
For more information visit Nfbpublishing.com

Preface

The stories told in this book took place over two years, from 2020-2022, and through a series of phone and in-person conversations between my mother and myself. Our conversations were recorded, transcribed, and written into story format. It was important for me to preserve these interactions in the manner in which they took place and in the way the stories were told by my mom, Roula Santamas. I believe this format truly captured her memory of experiences and her true nature.

Some of you reading this memoir may have been present during some of the events laid out in the book. Your experiences may be different than those of Roula's. I respect and honor your recollections and I look forward to hearing your stories in the future.

You may be mentioned by name in some of the stories told. Consider yourself one of the lucky ones who were able to personally engage with Roula over the years. Remember, the stories were told honestly and not meant to offend.

When transcribing, I was reminded of the quote from author Anne Lamott, "You own everything that happened to you. Tell your stories. If people wanted you to write warmly about them, they should have behaved better."

YiaYia Gets a New Knee

We had just settled into bed. Mom was resting as comfortably as could be expected in the hospital bed that Dad used to sleep in before he passed away this past August. I was in the bed right next to her, occupying the bed where Mom used to sleep, while caring for my father up until the last six days of his life. "It's comfortable," she says, "It makes me feel like I'm wrapped up in a cocoon." Having just come home from the hospital, following a total knee replacement, it was Mom's turn to be taken care of now by me, after having put off her knee surgery for over two years to care for my dad full-time. The pain

Cousin Androulla, Roula, Sister Goulla

pills were finally kicking in for Mom, making her drowsy. I needed no assistance falling asleep, as I was quickly learning that being a full-time caretaker was exhausting.

Suddenly, we were startled by the ringing of Mom's cell phone. I jumped up out of bed to answer. It was my cousin, Petros, calling from Las Vegas. His Cypriot dialect came through, at first, then quickly switched to broken English when he realized it was me. He said, "Androulla died. Tell your mother to call my mother. She is very upset and is crying." We calculated the seven-hour time difference in our heads and realized that it would be 5:00 a.m. in Cyprus. I turned on a lamp and used the remote control for the hospital bed to elevate my mom's upper body. She instructed me to get the house phone and my Theia Goulla's phone number from the rolodex in the kitchen. She would call her older sister immediately after hearing about the passing of their dear cousin, Androulla, in Cyprus. Greek/Cypriot conversation immediately began as the two sisters helped to console one another. Their conversation faded into the background as my mom's cell phone began to ring again. I answered. It was my mom's younger brother, Marios. He had just heard the news and was calling to let us know. I told him that Petros had just called and that Mom was on the phone with Goulla.

It took some time for us to settle back down following the startling and sad news. However, exhaustion for me and hydrocodone for mom eventually took over as we drifted off to sleep. It was 5:00 a.m. the following morning when I heard Mom wrestling with her walker and making her way to the bathroom. I sat up and rubbed the sleep from my eyes. When returning from the bathroom, she sat in a chair in the bedroom while I went to the kitchen to get her medicine, a glass of water, and her coffee. When I returned, I noticed that she was crying. I got her a tissue and gave her a hug. While sobbing, she said, "We were all raised together like orphans. None of us had our fathers growing up. Lefteri and Marianna didn't even have a mother. We were raised like orphans by your YiaYia Athena, Theia Eleni, and my YiaYia Mariannou, all in the same house. There were eight of us..." Her distant memories and her voice trail off as her attention is brought to the present moment.

Soon thereafter, the realization hit me, as I am sure it did my mom, on that one particular January morning in 2020. Most of the senior members of our family have already passed and those who remain are one year closer to death. The yearning to tell my mom's story while she is still willing and able to recall the events that unfolded in her one and only fascinating and precious life sits well with my soul.

Dedication

Here I offer you a glimpse into the lives of the generation of women who came before me and the sacrifices that they made for the sake of their children and their families. These are their backstories, as told through my mother's recollection and reflections. The tales are interwoven and the commonalities reflect the character of subsequent generations of women from my mother's side of the family, including myself. Although over the years I have heard bits and pieces of some of the stories that will be told in this memoir and family history, it hasn't been until now that, through my mother's eyes, the stories will unfold in a sequential order and shed light on the true character and resilient nature of Stavroula (Roula) Panayides-Santamas.

Top left to right: Athena Vassiliades-Panayides, Eirini Vassiliades, Eleni Vassiliades Bottom left to right: YiaYia Mariannou, Proyiayia Elengou

Whether we know it or not, we transmit the presence of everyone we have ever known, as though by being in each other's presence we exchange our cells, pass on some of our life force, and then we go on carrying that other person in our body, not unlike springtime when certain plants in fields we walk through attach their seeds in the form of small burrs to our socks, our pants, our caps, as if to say, "Go on, take us with you, carry us to root in another place." This is how we survive long after we are dead. This is why it is important who we become, because we pass it on."

— Natalie Goldberg, *Long Quiet Highway: Waking Up in America*

The Wonder Years: A Summary

It wasn't too long after I had returned back home to Elma, New York that I came across a post on Facebook. A workshop on writing family histories and memoirs was about to begin in the neighboring town of East Aurora, New York. This was surely a "sign" that reassured me that writing my mom's story was indeed the path I needed to be on. I immediately signed up for the class and told my mom that I was going to document her life story for a writing class that I was going to be taking. I made it seem as though she was my homework assignment. She immediately obliged and we set up our first phone call for February 2, 2020.

A Blonde is Born

My mom, Stavroula (Roula) Panayides was born on May 6, 1942, in Larnaca, Cyprus. The third largest island in the Mediterranean Sea, it is located south of Turkey, west of Syria and Lebanon, north of Israel, the Gaza Strip and Egypt, and Southeast of Greece.

Although Roula, her family, and the majority of the population of Cyprus were Greek Cypriot and of the Greek Orthodox faith, 18 percent of the population was made up of Turkish Cypriots. Roula was the second born daughter to Petros and Athena Panayides. Roula's father, my Pappou, Petros Panayides, was in the British army at the time of her birth. During WWII, as well as 25 years earlier in 1914, when the Mediterranean island was annexed by the UK, Cyprus served as a naval station as well as an important supply and training base for the British military.

Roula with father Petros Panayides.

Although there was a Cyprus Regiment supporting the British during WWII, especially after the invasion of Greece in 1940, Petros' role in the war and his length of service is unknown. Perhaps what Petros was better known for was his career as a residential painter. Roula's mother, my YiaYia Athena Panayides, supplemented and at times supported the family income by working tirelessly as a seamstress for wealthy families.

From her first-hand accounts of growing up on the island, for the first 17 years of her life, Roula admits, her blonde hair, green eyes, and adventurous personality became the center of attention and caused quite a stir among the locals in the village.

The Early Years

I begin by asking, "What do you know about your father being in the war when you were born?"

I know that my father was in the army when I was born. Because I was blonde, they used to joke with my mother that she had me with a German soldier. The Germans must have been around, too, at that time.

I ask Mom, "What are your first memories of growing up in Cyprus?"

In 1951, my father left for Australia to work as a painter. There were more opportunities there for him to earn money for our family. In addition, he had family, including a sister, in Australia already, which made it easier for him to move there. Before that, however, we were living in this big house in a Turkish neighborhood. When we lived there, we played with the Turkish kids. We were friends with them. I also remember a blind Turkish lady that lived next door to us. Even though she was blind, she was able to sew. She had names for all of the kids in the neighborhood. She called me "Jasmine." I would hear her calling me out loud and I would go to her house and help her thread her needles. I remember her house was always dark. Of course, she didn't need light to see anything, because she was blind.

In this big house, we were living together with my whole family. There were bedrooms upstairs where my Theia (Aunt) Eleni, Theio (Uncle) Kyriakos, my cousin Androulla, and my YiaYia (grandmother) Mariannou were living. My mother and father, my sister Goulla, my brother Marios, and I were living in a downstairs area that had one big, huge bedroom. I remember our beds were all lined up in this room. One night while we were sleeping, I woke up and saw the Virgin Mary at the foot of my bed. She was looking at me. I told my family about this, but nobody believed me. The Virgin Mary must have been looking out for me.

My mother had to cook outside in a courtyard. I remember there was running water in the middle of this courtyard. My father would go and wash himself out there. It was weird how we grew up living there.

We used to go to St. Lazarus church a lot with my YiaYia Mariannou. It was right in our neighborhood. Every time they had a funeral, my YiaYia Mariannou would take me and my sister, Goulla. We would light a candle and be there to pay our respects to the people who died.

Wanting to know more. I ask, "What do you remember about your father during this time?"

My father worked as a painter and he would come home tired and hungry. I remember he ate a lot. When we were sick, my mother wouldn't eat for days because she was so upset. My father, on the other hand, would sit down to eat. My mother would comment about his appetite. He would respond to her, "Do you want me to starve and die just because the kids are sick?" My mother would always get on him about his eating and his drinking, at least his drinking later in life.

The Middle Years

In 1951, we took my dad to the port in Limassol to get on the Hellenic Prince and leave
for Melbourne, Australia. I don't know who
took us or how we got there, but I remember
we all went and said goodbye. I didn't see him
after that for almost 20 years. My sister Goulla
was eleven years old and my brother Marios
was six years old at the time. I must have been
eight and a half. We were left without our father and my mother had the responsibility of
raising three children. She was tough on us.

We didn't like it at the time. She was cau-
tious and in charge. Aside from her mother

Goulla, Marios, Roula

(Mariannou), her sister (Eleni), and her brother (Vasso), she didn't have a husband that she could depend on.

My mom worked as a seamstress to supplement the family income. I guess
my father was sending us only 20 pounds a month from Australia, which
wasn't a lot of money. She followed in the footsteps of her mother, my YiaY-
ia Mariannou, who was also a seamstress. My mother would go to rich people's homes and sew for them all day. I remember the rich people would send
drivers to our house to pick her up. Sometimes she would take me with her,
especially if they had young children that I could play with. She also made all
of our clothes. My Theia Eirini used to send us fabric from Africa. My mother
used to make us the most unusual dresses from this fabric. You know, I was
just talking to your Uncle Marios the other day. We grew up happy. After our
father left, we never felt like we were deprived of anything. Our mother never

let us go hungry and she always worked hard to make sure that we had a good education. She took good care of us the best way she knew how.

After my father left for Australia, my mother moved my brother, sister, and me to a different home a couple of blocks away from the big house and our other family members. This was an apartment (commonly known as a "flat") that was located above the Stoa, an open area with businesses, shops, and the main bus stop in Larnaca. This was a very busy area. All of these little buses would come from different villages and would drop people off for the day to either shop or work. Then they would pick the people back up at the end of the day to take them home to their villages. We would sit on the veranda and watch everything.

When my mother wasn't working, she would pack a picnic and we would go to the Finikoudes Beach in the afternoon and hang out by the medieval castle. We would swim, eat, and then come home. My father wasn't around then so it must have been after he left.

During this time, YiaYia Mariannou and the rest of the family stayed in the big house. In the summer of 1955, my Theia Eirini came from Cameroon, Africa. She brought her children with her to Cyprus with the intention of leaving them to live with and be cared for by YiaYia Mariannou and Theia Eleni. Theia Eirini went back to Africa to be with her husband, Andreas, and to work. My cousin Marianna was still a baby, eight months old, when Theia Eirini brought them to Cyprus. Marianna's brother, my cousin Lefteri, was around six years old. I guess there were all kinds of diseases over there in Africa and the climate wasn't good for the kids. So, she made the decision to bring them home to be looked after. She went back to Africa to work and only returned to Cyprus once to see her children. She unfortunately got sick and she died in Africa.

In order to gain some clarity on these events, I messaged Marianna on Facebook and asked her what she remembers about her mother. Marianna, recalls, "I remember my stroller. It had a very light brownish colour with a tent on it (like an umbrella) for the sun. And just one scene remained in my memory of my mother pushing the stroller with me. My father came again when I was five years old, but alone, not with my mother. Someone had to stay in their job or perhaps the airplane ticket was too expensive from Africa. My mother, Eirini, died in Cameroon, Africa, on March 5, 1966."

Even though we had moved to the Stoa, we still lived close to my cousins. I remember playing with Marianna and Lefteri. Marianna was like our little sister or more like a little doll. I would take jasmine flowers and use a needle to put them on a string to make a circle of flowers. I would place it in Marianna's hair.

I must have been 13 or 14 when the British government closed the schools in Larnaca because of the war. My mother didn't want us, especially my brother, to fall behind on our studies. She was working hard to save money so that she could send my brother to college. But first, he had to finish high school. Goulla didn't want to go anywhere. So our mother arranged to have some tutoring done at home in Larnaca, for her and some of her friends. Because Marios was only twelve at the time, I went to Lefkara with him to look after him and to finish off the school year. Lefkara is about an hour and a half away from Cyprus. We used to vacation there often, even when my father was still around. It had a higher elevation than Larnaca, making it cooler there in the summer. Sometimes we would stay there for the entire summer. Because of this, my mother had connections there. She reached out to a lady that we used to rent from when we vacationed there. My mother offered to pay her to house us for the rest of the school year. There were other kids from Larnaca staying there as well. I remember that it was winter time and it was freezing.

The only problem were these guys...guys always liked me for some reason. They would sing to me underneath our balcony during the night. The neighbors were getting upset and complaining to the lady that was housing us. She told my mother that we couldn't stay there anymore. My mother was always mad at me because guys were always flirting with me. I wasn't doing anything bad. I didn't ask them to flirt with me. All I would do is stand on the balcony and the boys would go by on their bicycles. I would wave to them. That's all. Then they would serenade me. That's the way it was. You didn't date, you didn't talk to them, or meet them anywhere.

Eventually, my mother found another place that would take us, where an older lady lived. So, we went and stayed with her. Marios was with me and I had to help him take a bath. There was no bathtub in this house. Just a big tub. I had to heat up water from the stove so that we could bathe. But it was better after we started to stay with this other lady. The boys didn't bother me at this house. We stayed there a few months to finish out our school year. But we would come home on the weekends. We would go back and forth on the little village buses.

All in all, we had a good time while we were there. There was this teacher at the school in Lefkara. I don't remember his name but I do remember that he was funny. He used to teach us Greek dances. Because I did so well, he would put me in the front of the circle to lead the others.

I ask, "What other activities did you participate in at school?"

Back in Larnaca I played basketball and did the long-jump in the sand. I think I remember being good in gymnastics, too. We were in plays at school. We would go up on stage and say poems during the holidays. I guess I liked school. Although I never graduated.

For this school photo, Roula is positioned in the top row, 5th in from the left.

The Later Years

After a while, I don't know why, but we moved again. We all ended up back together in another house. We moved closer to the ocean. It was a big house with a lot of bedrooms. We lived with my cousins, Lefteri, Marianna, and Androulla. Also, with my Theia (Aunt) Eleni, and YiaYia (Grandmother) Mariannou. Androulla's father, my Theio (Uncle) Kyriakos, died of jaundice. He was yellow. He must have had liver problems. He was quite a bit older than Theia Eleni. Of course, my father was still in Australia. It was all women raising us.

I would sing around the house. My YiaYia Mariannou used to like it and would ask me to sing. She used to call me "Stavroula Mou." She was the only one that ever called me by my full name.

We shared one big kitchen, but everybody did their own cooking for their families. My mother would cook for us and Theia Eleni would cook for the others. On the weekends, my mother used to make us pastichio (noodles layered with ground beef and onions, finished off with a thick creamy bechamel sauce, and baked to a golden perfection). It was a treat. During the week we would eat beans, like faki (lentils and rice with caramelized onions). She made keftedes (fried meatballs). Not too much meat, however. Once in a while we'd have a roast or chicken. She made soup a lot: avgolemono (soup where the broth is thickened with egg and lemon juice. It is often served with boiled chicken) and trahana (a mixture of dried grain with fermented yogurt or milk). We'd have halloumi (Cypriot semi-hard goat/sheep cheese) and eggs. I guess we were already eating the Mediterranean diet way back then.

My uncle, Theio Vasso, would come and visit. He was the only father figure we had in our lives. We didn't have anybody else. He would take us to the beach. He loved to swim. I have memories of walking to the ocean to go swim-

Theio Vasso Vassiliades

ming with him. He was nice to us. He even took me one time to the mountains. I don't know why he only took me and not anybody else. He liked to travel and to go places. He had a good job. He worked for the Cyprus Broadcasting Corporation. He would translate and write the text of the nightly news for the broadcaster. He lived in Nicosia when he worked at the station. He learned without going to school. He taught himself. He used to borrow books from his rich friends and would read and study on his own. He was very smart...a brain.

We often went to parties, too. Well, I didn't go too much, but my sister did. My mother didn't want me to go for some reason. I don't know why. Goulla was going to all of these parties with her friends. Her friends would say, "Bring your sister, too." She didn't want to, but she took me with her to a couple of parties. She didn't like that her friends were paying a lot of attention to me.

So, that's why I decided to get out of there, get married, and leave. I'd had enough with everybody. Goulla didn't get married until after me. That's another thing. The people were saying to my mother, "Why are you going to marry the younger one before the older one?" My mother was debating if she would let me go or not. Theio Vasso, I think, talked her into it. No, my sister, Goulla didn't get married until three or four years after me.

But before I got married, I went to prison...

I immediately stopped my mom and announced that the story about her going to prison would be saved for another time. Also, I knew that there were a couple of other events that took place during this time period that I had heard over the years. I wanted her to expand upon these stories first, before her prison story. She agreed by commenting, "I'm really tired." Who's to blame her? After all, Mom had been reflecting on her life, growing up in Cyprus, for over thirty minutes.

Determined

It is Valentine's Day, Friday February 14, 2020. I take the three-hour drive to Youngstown, Ohio, from Elma, New York to check in on my mom, who is just shy of six weeks out of knee replacement surgery. My husband, Brian, accompanies me on the trip. My eldest son, Dylan, who attends Case Western Reserve University, in Cleveland, Ohio, takes a one-and-a-half-hour drive to Youngstown to have dinner with us and to check in on his YiaYia as well. After dinner, my mom rolls up her pant leg to show off her scar. With confidence she announces, "The physical therapists say that I'm determined. They all agree that by now, most of their knee replacement patients have screamed, at least once, during their therapy. I haven't screamed yet, but boy do they beat me up!"

I've been reflecting on my mom's statement, since returning home to Elma. While some may see my mom, Roula, as determined. This is just one of the many character traits cultivated in Roula, whether by choice or not, starting at a very young age. After hearing her stories and the series of events that took place in Roula's life, one may describe her not only as determined, but strong, brave, resilient, or even perhaps a little stubborn at times.

Next Time Put Me Under

This is something that I will never forget. It was one of the worst nightmares of my life...

When I was a young girl in Cyprus, I used to get a lot of head colds. By the time I was eight years old, the doctor said that my tonsils had to come out. My mother was given two choices. I could stay in Larnaca, where the doctor would put me under anesthesia to perform the surgery. Or, I could go to Nicosia, where the doctor would perform the surgery using only a local anesthetic. My mother didn't want me to go under anesthesia, for fear that I would never wake up. Because my father must have already been in Australia by this time, my mother made the decision, on her own, to send me to Nicosia. I had to stay overnight in a hotel after the surgery, so that I could be close to the doctor, in case of an emergency. My grandmother (YiaYia Mariannou) went with me, while my mother stayed home in Larnaca to care for my brother and sister.

When it was time for the surgery, they put me in this room where there was all of these knives and scissors laid out on a table. Because I was little, the nurse sat in a chair with me on her lap. I think they tied my hands up to the chair. They asked me if I wanted to be blindfolded. But what did I know at eight years old? So, I told them "No." Looking back, I wish I would have said "yes" to the blindfold. So, now I'm watching everything with huge eyes! This doctor began putting shots in my throat to numb me. I watched him putting scissors in my mouth to start cutting. Then all of the sudden, I heard "clip, clip!" It didn't hurt but I could see and hear everything. Next thing you know, I see one tonsil lands on the table. Then the other one. After they removed the tonsils, they must have had to cauterize my throat. All I could smell was my burning flesh. After they were done, they asked me if I wanted to take my tonsils home in a glass jar. I said, "No!"

When it was over, my YiaYia and I ended up in the hotel. I was supposed to eat a lot of cold food, like ice cream. However, I remember the hotel making me mashed potatoes to eat. I don't know if the hot mashed potatoes did it or not, but I started to bleed. I ended up back at the doctor the next day. They had to cauterize my throat, again! All of this just because my mother didn't want me to go under anesthesia. Now, every time I go to the dentist and they tell me to open my mouth, that terrifying image pops into my mind. Since then, any surgical procedure I've ever had, I tell them, "Put me under!"

Strong Women Raise Strong Daughters

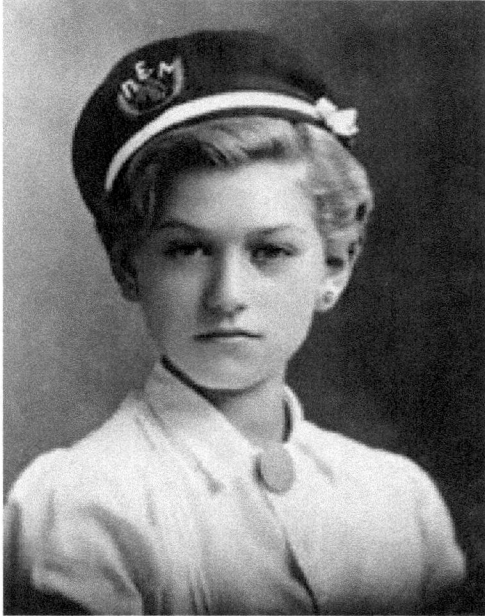

My mother was very stern and strict with me, not with my sister or brother. I was a middle child and it's true what they say about middle children. My older sister, Goulla, never did anything wrong, and neither could my younger brother, Marios. Of course, he was the youngest and the only boy. He always got away with a lot. Not me...

There was a field trip being planned at school that I was looking forward to going on. We were told to bring our bathing suits because we were going to have time to swim in the ocean

Roula after her haircut.

as part of the field trip. My mother didn't want to let me go because of this. She finally gave in and let me go. But she said, "No way" to the bathing suit. I snuck it on the field trip anyways. When I came home, my mother knew what I had done because she found my wet bathing suit. Like I said before, she was always mad at me. However, I was in high school at the time and old enough to make my own decisions.

Not like when I was younger and she forced me to get my hair cut because she didn't want me to be pretty anymore. She dragged me to this Turkish lady's house. I don't even know if she was a beautician. That was a sad day for me. I didn't want to show my face anywhere for weeks. There are not too many pictures of me with my hair that short. I kept my hair long for many years after that experience. She didn't want the boys to like me. That's why she had my hair cut short. Oh, but they still liked me...

The Serenading Bicyclists

I was very close to my cousin, Androulla. Even though we went to different schools, we were the same age, separated by just a couple of months. When the English Government closed the public schools in Larnaca, Androulla applied and got into the private American Academy. She must have been smarter than me. I applied but didn't get in. So, she stayed in Larnaca and attended the American Academy while I went to the school in Lefakara to finish off my year. Even though we each had different groups of friends from school, we lived together during high school. On the weekends, we would hang out. On Sundays after church, in the early afternoon, we would go to the Finikoudes. We would walk back and forth to pass the time.

> *Irene: I think back to the times that I have been to the Finikoudes, once when I was seventeen and again in my early twenties. I would walk along the beach on the palm tree lined promenade. I imagine that it hasn't changed much since my mom frequented this area. I too enjoyed hanging out with both the locals and the tourists. While on Holiday, I spent most of my time here at the Finikoudes sunning myself on the beach, eating, and flirting with the Cypriot boys.*

Mom continues: As I mentioned earlier, the main mode of transportation for the boys on the island, even through high school, were bicycles. Nobody had a car back then. On our way home from the Finikoudes one day, these guys started following us on their bicycles. While following us, they began to sing to us. You know, I was a blond and my cousin, Androulla, had dark eyes. There was a Greek song with lyrics, "Xanthia Kai Mavra Matia," translated, the blond and black eyes. They followed us the whole way home, riding their bikes and singing this song to us.

EOKA

April 1, 1955, marks the start of EOKA (Ethniki Organosis Kypri-
on Agoniston). EOKA was a Greek Cypriot nationalist guerilla orga-
nization that formed a resistance movement in an effort to fight for
the end of British rule in Cyprus and for the island's right to self-de-
termination and eventual union with Greece (Enosis). The EOKA
organization had at its core adopted Greek national ideologies that
included religious, conservative, and anti-communist ideals. EOKA
members consisted of guerilla mountain groups who lived in hidden
camps in the forests in addition to a broader national front of Greek
Cypriot citizens.

Roula's Theio Avgoustis Efstathiou

One of the most important battles that occurred between the Greek Cypriot guerillas and the British was called The Battle of Machairas. It took place on March 2 and 3, 1957, in the Troodos mountains, near the monastery of Machairas. This highly publicized battle, due to the crowds of reporters that came, had become highly scrutinized by the world. At the center of this battle was Roula's uncle, her father's half-brother, Avgoustis Efstathiou. Participating in this battle that lasted over ten hours, Avgoustis, was one of four guerillas hidden in a cave alongside Grigoris Afxentiou, who was second in command in the EOKA movement. Upon being found by the British, they were asked to surrender. Although refusing to do so himself, Afxentiou forced the other four guerillas to vacate the cave without him. Upon realizing that Afxentiou was not one of their prisoners, the British immediately went into the cave, only to be retaliated by gunfire that would end up killing one of the British soldiers. Avgoustis was sent back into the cave to try and convince Afxentiou to surrender. However, he ended up staying in the cave, battling side by side with Afxentiou. Eventually, the British poured large amounts of gasoline into the cave. While Avgoustis Efstathiou was able to escape, emerging from the cave on fire, Afxentiou burned to death. While the guerrillas fought in the mountains, the British recruited Turkish Cypriots to become police officers, in an effort to assist them in their retaliation against the Greek Cypriot community. EOKA would push back by recruiting Greek Cypriot citizens and school children who would participate in demonstrations, riots against the police, and distribution of propaganda. In an effort to assist the guerilla fighters, who were considered the backbone of this movement, the Greek Cypriot citizens provided them with intelligence, supplies, weapons, medicines, recruits, and safe houses.

Roula recalls, "My mother's cousin, Noni, was very much involved in these activities. We were living in the apartment above the Stoa. One night, I don't know what he did, but the police were running after him. He ended up climbing over our balcony and onto our veranda. My mother was really scared. She ended up opening the door for him and hiding him in our apartment. He was never arrested for whatever he did that night, but he was always getting himself into trouble." With two family members actively involved in EOKA, Roula's uncle Avgoustis and Athena's cousin Noni, the Panayides house was always under watch by the British.

On the 45-year anniversary of the start of the resistance movement, April 1, 2020, Roula's brother, Marios, vividly recalls, "I started seventh grade in September of 1955. It was my first year of high school in Cyprus. In November of 1955, several bombs were thrown at the British by students from our high school, killing one of their soldiers. The British closed our school. Our school in Larnaca was one of the first schools in Cyprus to be shut down. That's when my mother sent me to Lefkara to go to school."

By February of 1956, after one boy was shot dead by a British soldier, the island's school system was shut down almost completely. Marios explains, "I remained in Lefkara, going to school with my sister, Roula, for at least a year or two. It was when we returned from Lefkara, that I took 'the oath' to support the EOKA movement. During this time, my sister Roula, who had also taken 'the oath,' became a war hero, 'by default.'"

Stavroula and the Case of Mistaken Identity

During the war, I remember going to a friend's house with a bunch of my fellow classmates in order to take 'the oath.'

> I interrupt mom, "I found 'the oath.'" She responds, "What? How did you find it?" I reply, "On the internet, of course. Would you like to hear it?" Mom says, "Yes, of course."

> The EOKA Youth Organization oath is as follows:
> I swear in the name of the Holy Trinity that:
> I shall work with all my power for the liberation of Cyprus from the British yoke sacrificing for this even my life;
> I shall perform without objection all the instructions of the organization which may be entrusted to me and I shall not bring any objection, however difficult and dangerous these may be;
> I shall not abandon the struggle unless I receive instructions from the leader of the organization and after our aim has been accomplished;
> I shall never reveal to anyone any secret of our organization neither the names of my chiefs nor those of the other members of the organization even if I am caught and tortured;
> I shall not reveal any of the instructions, which may be given me even to my fellow combatants.
> If I disobey my oath, I shall be worthy of every punishment as a traitor and may eternal contempt cover me.

Roula: My part in EOKA consisted mostly of distributing flyers. We would meet at a main house. It was here where we would get our instructions and our flyers. The girls that were involved would put rubber bands around their legs. We would hide the flyers there, underneath our dresses and skirts. On Sundays, during church services, the girls would hang out in the balcony of the church, mostly to socialize. After we took our oath, we were given instructions to throw the flyers down from the balcony to the people attending the church service. We tried not to bring attention to ourselves. However, one day we were out on the street protesting in a group. The police threw tear gas at us to break us up.

My mother suspected that I was doing things to support EOKA. My brother Marios was also participating. I'm not sure how much my sister was involved. She was always scared to do things. I was more of a rebel.

It must have been around 1956 or 1957. We were all living in the big house by the ocean with Theia Eleni, Androulla, YiaYia Mariannou, Marianna, and Lefteri. On this particular night, my Theio Vasso was staying with us. We had all gone to bed. Sometime very early in the morning, we were startled by banging on our door. Theio Vasso got up to answer it. There must have been four or five British soldiers at the door. They demanded they search our house. We had no choice but to let them in. We were all so scared. There was a storage area half-way up our stairs. I remember them going through it, as well as the rest of the house. We had no idea at the time what they were looking for. Whatever it was, they couldn't find it.

Then the soldiers looked at me and told me that I had to go with them. There was nothing my family could say or do to keep this from happening. These were hostile times. I stayed in the Larnaca jail for one day. I was then transported close to Nicosia to a village called Ormideia. This was the main jail, where the British put all of their prisoners. They started interrogating me, asking me all sorts of questions. There was a good guy and a bad guy. Although they were British, they spoke to me in Greek. There were Turkish guards there, too. There was a Turkish lady who was assigned to look after me. She was nice. I think she felt sorry for me. I was in a cell, alone, with a bucket to use as a toilet. Later I learned that Theio Vasso rode his bicycle to Ormideia. He had a blanket, pillow, and other things that would help to make me more comfortable. They wouldn't let him give those things to me.

They questioned me for several days. They kept asking me where the gun was and who killed the general? I kept repeating the same thing over and over, "I don't know, I don't know, I don't know." Apparently, a British General was killed on one of the main streets in Larnaca. They were looking for the girl who hid the gun used in the killing. She was also a blond, her name was Stavroula, and she was my age! What finally made them realize that they had the wrong person was when they asked me if I had a sister named Maria. I told them, "No, my sister is named Georgia." I think at that moment they started to realize that they had the wrong Stavroula. Then it hit me. I knew who they were looking for. However, I didn't say anything to them, because I took the oath...

I was finally brought back to Larnaca. But they didn't release me right away. I stayed there for another day or two. It wasn't so bad being in the Larnaca jail. I could communicate with other people I knew that were being arrested around the same time as me. Not like the jail in Ormideia. When I was there, I could hear people getting tortured screaming and crying. I remember they once let me go outside to empty my bucket. I saw guys lined up along a wall with their hands in the air, wearing only their underwear. They were torturing them, trying to get information out of them. They didn't torture me that way. They only shone bright lights in my eyes while they were questioning me.

I was finally released from jail. There was no way to communicate with my family that I was being released, so I started walking home, alone, along the Finikoudes. A neighbor drove by and saw me walking. He stopped and gave me a ride home. I walked in the door and I remember saying, "I need a bath!" Everybody was so happy to see me. They started asking me so many questions while my mother started warming up the bath water for me. Funny thing, while I was taking my bath, I decided to shave my legs. Still trembling from the whole ordeal, I had cut a big chunk out of my leg with the razor. Afterwards, when my family saw the bad cut, they started freaking out. They thought this had happened to me in jail. I remember having that scar for years. Afterwards all my friends though that I was a hero. However, my mother still kept a tight rein on me. I think she was ready to marry me off by this time. She wanted me to be somebody else's problem!

It was after Roula's arrest and release that her Uncle Avgoustis was eventually captured by the British during the Battle of Machairas. He was thrown in the same jail where Roula had been a prisoner for a couple of days in the village of Ormideia. In his jail cell, he kept a photo of his niece, Roula. During his imprisonment, one of the other prisoners commented to Avgoustis, "You know her too?" I guess Roula, 'by default,' had unknowingly become famous among the prisoners, as well as with her friends in Larnaca.

Roula's mother, Athena, was Avgoustis' only family in Cyprus, with his half-brother having left for Australia many years prior. His sister-in-law, Athena, would go and visit him there as often as she could. On one of her visits, she was wearing a black dress. Avgoustis told her, "Don't wear black again. The next color I want to see you wear is white. Freedom is coming soon."

Finally, on December 5, 1958, the foreign ministers of Greece and Turkey, compromised on a solution. The London-Zurich Agreement was created and resulted in Cyprus becoming an independent and sovereign country.

A Marriage to Last Forever

The last six days of my dad's life were spent in the hospital and in a Hospice care facility. Mom spent each of those last days by his side, day after day, night after night, only running home to shower and grab a quick bite to eat for a couple of hours each day. Often, my cousin Sue, Uncle Marios, brothers, and I had to force her to leave, reassuring her that we were ok to stay with dad and that she should take her time. On one of those days, My Uncle Marios and I were left in Dad's care. After Mom left, an overwhelming amount of silence permeated through the room at Hospice House. It was eventually broken by my Uncle Marios. "Do you realize that when your dad was working the 3-11 shift at the steel mill, your mom used to wait up for him and cook him a fresh meal to have when he got home? I would remember her frying pork chops or roasting a chicken at 10 o'clock at night. She spent her whole married life taking care of him. She knows no other way."

As August 23, 2019, my mom and dad's 60th wedding anniversary quickly approached, so did my dad's final days. Mom was pleading, "Please, I just want him to make it to our 60th wedding anniversary." Sadly, just one day shy of this notable event, on August 22, 2019, at 01:23 a.m., Dad passed away peacefully in his sleep with my mom sleeping comfortably in a cot right next to him.

THE ARRANGEMENT

The scheduled phone calls between my mom and me where I ask her questions about her past and record her stories on my I-Pad, while talking to her on speaker phone, have pretty much become bi-monthly occurrences for the two of us. Despite the fact that I have been speaking to her daily since I moved to Buffalo thirty years ago, I set these phone calls up with her during our morning call, giving her advance notice about what it is that I want to learn more about either later that same day or the next. This conversation would be the second out of four that we would have on this particular day, Tuesday, April 20, 2020.

"Tell me how you met dad," I ask.

It was the summer before my last year of high school. We went to elementary school for six years and then high school for six years. I had just finished my fifth year of high school. I had one more year left before graduating. I don't know how it all came about exactly. But, Avgie, who was married to Demos' older brother, Fidos, was the one who arranged everything. She was the one who explained to my mother and YiaYia Mariannou that her brother-in-law, Demos, was visiting from the United States and they wanted to find him a wife. Demos' sister, your Theia Lygia, and her son, your cousin George, who was five at the time, were also visiting from the United States. Lygia was adamant that your dad finds a wife before returning to the United States. Who knows why? Maybe he was running around with girls there and causing his sisters, Lygia and Eglie, problems. That was the story I heard, anyways.

Avgie talked it over, first, with my family. Then my family talked to me. They told me that this guy, Demos Santamas, wants to marry you and take you to the United States. Then Demos came over to our house with his parents and Avgie. I guess Demos had already seen me before in a picture. He was shown a picture of me and of my sister, Goulla. But he liked me best, because of my long blonde hair. That was his initial attraction. Up until then, I was interested in a couple of boys. You know, I would flirt with them. But my mother always put a stop to it. So at that time, I wasn't really interested in anybody. If I was, maybe I would have said no. I did have a choice. Nobody forced me to agree to this. But the idea of going to the United States appealed to me, at the time. I was 17, what did I know? I knew nothing about the United States except for the things that I saw in movies when I would go to the theatre. Anyways, I said OK and the wheels started turning. They invited my whole family to his house and we had a big dinner celebration with his whole family. We had to get ready for a wedding. Demos was supposed to go back to the United States. He was on a leave of absence from work and obligated to go back soon. We were getting married in two weeks!

The engagement party from left to right: YiaYia Susanna, Avgie, Lygia, Marios, Athena, YiaYia Christinou, Roula, George, Demos, Pappou Petros.

I didn't even have a wedding dress. I wasn't prepared for a wedding. So, Lygia got involved in getting me a dress. A year or two before, she had sent her husband's niece, who lived in a village in Cyprus, a wedding dress from the United States. Lygia realized that we were about the same size. So, we took a drive to the village. I tried it on and the dress fit me. I don't think that it needed any alterations. Even though it was a borrowed dress, it was pretty. I'm looking at my wedding picture now. Your father's niece, Maro, and my cousin, Marianna, were our flower girls. Up until then, I had never even worn make-up. Avgie told me that I needed some lipstick. I didn't even know how to put it on. Somebody had to do it for me. The first time I wore lipstick was on my wedding day.

I interrupt, "Were any of your other friends getting married?"

No. No. Nobody got married until after they finished high school. I was the first. I don't remember having a reception. It was customary to give each guest a cookie, Kourabiedes, after the ceremony. And that was it. We went to Nicosia and stayed in a hotel. That was my wedding night, which was scary. I don't want to get into the details but I was wondering what I had gotten myself into.

Flower girls: Maro(left) and Marianna(right) with Niki and YiaYia Mariannou peeking out from behind.

Roula and Demos honeymoon in Pedoulas Village.

When we got back to Larnaca, we decided to go to the mountains for our honeymoon. Lygia announced, "George and I want to go with you." She saw this as an opportunity to go up into the Troodos mountains. Although she promised that she wouldn't bother us once we got there, we stayed in the same hotel. Our rooms were right next door to each other. Georgie used to come over and knock on our door all the time. It was okay though. We had a good time. We would go for walks and go out to eat. We must have been there for a week. I have a lot of pictures somewhere from our time up in the mountains.

I remember a funny story from our honeymoon. The rooms had this pot under the bed that you would use to go pee in during the night. Georgie took the pot and put it on his head. Your dad took a picture of him. You should ask your cousin George about that. Maybe he has the picture.

It was tough for me. But your father was nice. He was gentle. Even though he was ten years older than me, he wasn't forcing himself on me or anything. Eventually, I learned what it was all about. Nobody ever talked to me about sex.

I never even talked about it with my girlfriends. We never really knew what was involved in a relationship between a man and a woman. Of course, my mother wasn't going to tell me anything. When we got back from our honeymoon, all of my girlfriends wanted to know the details. As I said, nobody really knew anything about sex. So, they had to learn it from me!!

It was time to get ready to go to the United States. I needed to get a passport and a chest x-ray. It was taking some time to get everything together. Longer than we had expected. Demos needed to get back to the United States for work. He even suggested leaving me in Cyprus until my travel documents were in order. However, my mother put her foot down, stating, "If you leave her behind, she will not be coming to the United States." She wasn't having any of it. Me having to travel to America alone. I'm not exactly sure what happened, but Demos managed to make arrangements to stay in Cyprus longer, until I was ready. We got married August 23, 1959. I think we left for the United States sometime in October. I can't remember the exact date.

Roula Santamas Arrives in America

We landed in New York City. From the airport, we took a taxi to a really nice hotel. One of the old hotels in New York City. I think it's still around, but I can't remember the name. Your dad made these arrangements for us. I didn't know anything about them. We stayed in New York for a day or two. Then we got on a train to Youngstown, Ohio. When we arrived in Youngstown, we stayed with Demos' sister, Eglie, her husband Paul, and their daughter Susie, who was almost two at the time. Eglie was really pregnant with your cousin Peter. It was here that my life in the United States really began.

I quickly found out that Demos was working all different shifts at the steel mill, Youngstown Sheet and Tube. He was working 3:00 p.m. to 11:00 p.m. and 11:00 p.m. to 7:00 a.m. He was getting ready one night at 10:00 p.m. I asked him where he was going. He said, "To work." All I knew about my husband was that he was from the United States and that he had a job. I didn't even know what kind of job he had.

We both chuckle as I comment, "Maybe you should have asked more questions."

Yes. Yes. All I knew was that he was the brother of Fidos Santamas. Fidos was a big deal in Cyprus. He was the president of the bank. The whole Santamas family was very well known. I didn't ask any questions.

My Theio Vasso was involved in the arrangement, too. My mother and YiaYia were asking his opinion. My YiaYia Mariannou didn't want me to go to the United States. She saw what happened when she sent her daughter, my Aunt Irene, to Africa, to get married. She told my mom, "Think twice before you do this. I sent my daughter far away and I'm sorry that I did."

Theio Vasso convinced them, however, that the Santamas' were a nice family. Plus, my mother still had another older daughter and a son to care for at home. My mother had to make all of the decisions for us, with my father having left so many years prior to got to Australia. I did learn later, however, that after she sent me to the United States, she was sorry that she did.

I had a hard time adjusting, too. I'm not going to lie. I think that if I wasn't so far away, like in England or someplace closer, I probably would have turned around and gone back home to Cyprus. I was lonely, especially those nights when he was working and I was all by myself. I was so scared.

Anyways, we stayed with Eglie for a short time before we found an apartment on the same street as her, on Florida Avenue. We rented a bedroom and a kitchen from a widow and her son. We all had to share the same bathroom. I guess she was a big help to me. She was nice and looked after me. I remember she'd have the TV on all day long. She would invite me downstairs to watch with her. I didn't understand anything. She would laugh and laugh and laugh at whatever she was watching. I couldn't figure out what was so funny. However, I spent most of my time upstairs, in my own bedroom and kitchen.

We lived in that apartment when your cousin, Peter K., was born. As I mentioned, Eglie was really pregnant with him when I arrived in the United States in October. On November 22, 1959, Paul walked down to our apartment and knocked on our door. He said, "I think Eglie is ready to have the baby." Paul didn't drive. So, we took them to the hospital. A few days later, it was Thanksgiving. Lygia cooked a turkey and brought it over to Eglie's house. Then we went to pick up Eglie and Peter from the hospital. We brought them home and I had my first Thanksgiving dinner. I remember your dad ate but then had to leave for work. He was working the 3:00 p.m. to 11:00 p.m. shift that day.

From then on, we always celebrated Thanksgiving and Peter's birthday at Eglie's house. Of course, we celebrated Christmas at Theia Lygia's house, because your cousin George's birthday was on Christmas Eve. I remember buying my first Christmas presents ever, for Georgie and Susie. I bought them matching cowboy and cowgirl outfits. Then, of course, every Easter, we were back at Theia Eglie's house to celebrate Susie's birthday on April 25. It wasn't until I had the three of you, that we started having family birthday parties that were not associated with any holiday.

Peter, George, Sue

We eventually bought our first house on Dewey Avenue. This is where we lived when all three of you were born.

I curiously asked, "Dewey Avenue was little bit further away from Theia Eglie. Did you feel even lonelier in this house?"

Not really. Your Theia Lygia used to get her friends, put them in her car, and drive all over. They would drop in on me all the time when we lived on Dewey Avenue. I would make them coffee. Theia Ioanna, Theia Dimitra, and Theia Fivi were three sisters. Lygia would take them shopping and drive them all around. Your Theia Lygia had freedom. She was married to Christ but she had money and freedom. She even had a new car.

I eventually brought my brother, your Uncle Marios, to the United States. He lived with us and was good company for me. He was a student at Youngstown State University. He would walk to the corner of Dewey Avenue and Market Street to catch the bus that went to the University. He stayed with us for about three years before leaving for St. Louis, to go to medical school.

I had a hard time, but I survived. I didn't know how to cook. I remember calling my mom and asking her for recipes and for advice on how to do things. They always got the time change mixed up. When the phone would ring at 5:00 a.m., I knew it was family calling from Cyprus. I remember the phone call that my mother made to me to tell me that my Theia Eirini (Aunt Irene) had died in Africa. I was pregnant with you and they didn't want to upset me. After you were born, and I found out that you were a girl, I named you after her.

I was in the United States for eight years, from 1959-1967. Your brother Pete was five, your brother Alki was three, and you were nine months old when your father and I decided to sell the house, pack everything up, and move back to Cyprus.

I stopped the recording as Mom and I decided that we had covered quite a bit this afternoon. Her return to Cyprus would be saved for next time. Before hanging up, my mom asked me, "Tell me again what you are doing with these recordings?" I explained to her that I was transcribing the interviews by hand, typing them into a story format onto my computer, and reading the stories, out loud, to a writing group that meets every Thursday.

I announce to my mom, "The ladies in the group are amazed by you. They want to meet you. They asked if I could bring you in for show and tell." She responds, "That's ridiculous. Why would they want to meet me? Besides, now they know all of the intimate details of my life. That's kind of embarrassing!"

A couple of hours had passed since our conversation. I started getting dinner ready when the phone began to ring. I noticed, on caller id, that it was Mom. Upon answering, she spoke, "I just remembered a couple of things I wanted to tell you that pertain to what we were talking about earlier. One story from before I left for the United States and one after I had arrived in the United States." I ask her to hold on a minute while I set up my I-pad to record and put her on speaker phone. "Ok, I'm all set," I tell her.

This is about the first time that I ever tasted pistachios. Did I ever tell you this story?

"No," I respond.

Your Pappou Petros, Demos' father, had these fields at his house with all kinds of stuff growing. We were at your daddy's house, I can't remember if it was before or after our wedding, but it was during that time. While we were sitting around and talking, Petros started picking these things off of a tree, peeling them, and giving them to me to eat. I asked him what they were and he said, "pistachios." They were so fresh, right from the tree. The outside shell hadn't even gotten hard yet. They were soft enough to peel. The inside was tender and soft, too. Not roasted, like we buy them here at the store. I had never even heard of pistachios before. This was a new experience for me.

I remember another story, too, about after I came to the United States. Your Theia Lygia threw a party for me. It was at her house. She introduced me to all of her friends. It was like a little welcome shower. I think some of her friends might have given me gifts, too. It was nice of her to gather all of her Cypriot friends and invite them over just to meet me. Lygia really took me under her wing. She was like a mother figure to me. Eglie, too, but Lygia was really looking after me. I think that she was probably one of the reasons that I survived. She was someone that I could depend on. She would take me places also. On some days, when your dad was working 3:00 to 11:00, he would drop me off at Lygia's house in Campbell. She lived close to the steel mill. This way, I wasn't home all by myself. Then Demos would pick me up after his shift at 11:00 o'clock at night. This was before I had kids.

Mom concludes by saying, "So that is all. I think this chapter is good for now."

Not quite yet, however. A couple more hours pass when the phone rings. I notice, once again, that it is my mom. It's around 8:30, a little late for her to be calling. I answer the phone.

Guess what? Alec (my mom's third eldest grandson) just called to tell me that he and Jessica got engaged today. What are the chances? I was just talking to you about my engagement and my wedding and Alec calls me, on the same day, to tell me about his engagement. However, they've been together for five years, three of which, they have spent living together. And who knows when their wedding will be? Their situation is a lot different from mine!

Motherhood

May is a very special time of year for my mom. Without fail, we travel to Ohio around this time, to celebrate her birthday on May 6 as well as Mother's Day, which normally falls just few days after her birthday. With no signs of the Covid 19 quarantine being lifted in New York State and May of this year quickly approaching, my son Dylan and I decided to break the "stay at home" orders and drive to Ohio to visit my mom, who has been cooped up alone in her house for almost two months. Aside from the bag of gifts that we purchased for her, we made the decision to bring her a "Kindle Fire" and my old "I-phone 7." They have been laying around the house, unused. My family agreed, if Mom had a Kindle, she would have an unlimited number of books available to her right at the tip of her fingers and wouldn't YiaYia love to FaceTime, get text messages, and photos from her family and grandkids? After all, her friend, Marlene, was just commenting on the phone the other day with my mom about how she loves both her Kindle and her I-phone. We had convinced ourselves, yet we knew the sensitivity of introducing these devices was going to be met with some resistance. So, we needed to wait for the perfect moment...

The next morning after our arrival, Mom announced that White House Farms was finally open, "I want you to make me scallops for dinner. You make the best scallops. We can go to White House Farms and get some of their homegrown asparagus to have with them. I need peanut butter, too. I like their peanut butter." Our options were limited in what we could do, due to the unseasonably cold weath-

er and where we could go, due to the closing of non-essential busi-
nesses, so we decided to take the nice twenty-minute drive to White
House Farms in Canfield, Ohio.

On our way there, I told Mom that we needed to continue our in-
terview process this weekend as well. I recalled where we left off. "We
need to talk about when you moved us all back to Cyprus."

She responded back, "I didn't have a chance to tell you about hav-
ing the three of you yet. Shouldn't we talk about that first?" Ponder-
ing why this was a huge oversight on my part, I answer, "Of course."

As I sit down to write, I reflect on something that I had read a few
days later, in honor of Mother's Day. Speaking of her own mother,
who has passed away, Maria Shriver writes, in her weekly Sunday
Paper, "I'd give anything for her to pull up a chair and sit down with
me—truly share with me—how she felt about being a mother and
grandmother. I'd like to think it was her greatest joy."

This is my chance, while my mother is still alive, to pull up a chair
and have my mom, who was barely out of childhood when she had
the three of us, describe to me what it felt like to become a mother.
Later that afternoon, after a brief lesson on the Kindle, we get comfy
on the couch. Mom, who is momentarily lost in thought, glances
upstairs towards the bedrooms and begins.

Do you know that we furnished our whole house on Dewey Avenue for
$1,000? After we moved into the house, we went to a store downtown that
Theia Lygia told us about, and we picked everything out. That bedroom set that
I still have upstairs in the spare bedroom, that was our original bedroom set.
It's from 1959. We also got everything for our living room: a couch, a chair, tables, lamps, and our kitchen table and chairs. Everything for $1,000. Of course,
your dad was only bringing home $250 in each paycheck. I think that was
every couple of weeks. So, $1,000 was a lot of money back then.

I ask, "Did you purchase this dining room set at the same time, as well?"

No, this dining room set that I have now, I bought from a neighbor on Dewey Avenue. The table with six chairs, buffet, and china cabinet cost only $55. And this secretary, I bought it from one of our neighbors, after we came back from Cyprus and moved on to Mistletoe. I think we paid about fifty bucks for it.

Roula pictured in dining room.

I comment, "The secretary has always been my favorite piece of furniture."

Mom replies, "Yes, you can take it whenever you want. Bring a U-Haul next time you come. Are you taping me right now?"

"Yes," I chuckle. "Just in case you tell me something important and I can't remember all of the details."

Mom continues: Another thing I remembered that I wanted to tell you. We used to go to a grocery store called Loblaws. It was your Theia Eglie's favorite grocery store. It was right at the end of her street, on Florida Avenue. We used to fill up an entire cart full of groceries for five dollars. Can you believe that? Now-a-days you can't even get a gallon of milk for five dollars. Or at least the organic milk that you buy!

*After some laughter at this comment about my shopping habits
and a brief moment of silence, I chime in, "You were 18 when you got
pregnant with Peter, right?"*

Let's see. He was born March 15, 1961, and I turned 19 on May 6 of that year. So, I was almost 19 when he was born. He was late. I was supposed to have him on March 3. I was afraid to stay at home by myself. So, when your dad went to work the 3:00 to 11:00 p.m. shift, he would take me to his sister, Lygia's, house. I was at her house when my water broke. She's the one who took me to the hospital. She must have contacted Demos at work and he met us at St. Elizabeth's Hospital. The doctor that Lygia told me to go to, that delivered your brother, wasn't even a gynecologist. He was just a regular doctor who delivered babies, too.

Actually, this lady from church was there, too. I didn't know her at the time but we met walking the hallways. It was Barbara Vouvalis. She had her son, Nick... Oh wait. She had Nick when I had your brother, Alki. I got confused. Let's finish with Peter.

I didn't know anything about taking care of babies. Lygia came over to help me give him a bath. We almost drowned your brother, Pete! I thought she knew what she was doing. I don't know how she managed to take care of George. After that incident, I told her that I could manage on my own.

After Peter was born, I took him to the same doctor who delivered him for a follow-up visit. He wasn't a pediatrician either. Peter's belly button was swollen up like a balloon. This doctor wanted to tie a string around it to cut off the circulation. When I heard that, I said, "No thank you." I never went to that doctor again for anything. It was Theia Joanna's daughter-in-law, Irene, who finally introduced me to a real pediatrician. There were two of them, Dr. Anderson and Dr. Wiltsy. I took Peter there and they put some medicine on his belly button. Eventually it dried up and fell of naturally. None of this nonsense about tying a string around Peter's belly button.

This same lady, Irene, also introduced me to her gynecologist. I can't remember his name, but he was a good doctor. He was a fat guy. He delivered both Alki on August 16,1963, and you on September 19, 1966, at North Side

Hospital. After having two boys, he knew that I wanted a girl... You know they would put you under when you had babies back then. They would put a gas mask over your face, you would take a deep breath, and you were out. Anyways, I went to the hospital to have you and when I woke up, the doctor was standing over me, smiling. He said, "You've got your girl!" He was a nice guy. I liked him a lot.

That other doctor, who delivered Peter, delivered Lygia and Eglie's babies. He was in Campbell and all of the Greeks went to him. Demos didn't know any better. So, I was listening to what his sisters were telling me to do at that time.

I interrupt, "Let's go back and talk about Alki's birth. Do you remember any of the details?"

Mom responds: "No, I don't remember too much about Alki being born." We both chuckle as I comment, "Oh boy. Wait until he hears this. No wonder the poor kid has suffered from middle child syndrome all of his life."

Wait. Wait. I remember your father taking me to the hospital. Lygia took care of Peter, while I delivered Alki. The only thing, Alki was born with a red birthmark on the side of his face. I was really upset by this. The staff at the hospital told me that the marks would eventually fade. But they never did fade completely. It was called "wine something." There's a name for it...

I looked it up quickly on my phone and determined that it was probably a "port wine stain."

Mom continues: One other thing about Alki. His skin turned yellow after a few days. They told me that he had yellow jaundice. The only thing that I remember about yellow jaundice was that Androulla's father, Theio Kyriakos, died of yellow jaundice. I got so scared then when they told me that Alki had it. However, they reassured me that Alki would be fine. They would take him and give him treatments every day. I think they would put him under a light.

Another thing with Peter, now that I am remembering. I got an infection, after I delivered him. You know, they used to cut you when you had a baby. So, they took him away from me for a few days. Until I got better, I couldn't nurse him.

And with you, everything went well. I didn't have any issues. After I had you, your dad brought your brothers to the hospital to see you. They weren't allowed to come into the room. I remember waving to them from the window.

Yup, I had my hands full with three kids at home.

Once again, silence emerges when I ask, "How did Peter react when you brought Alki home and then me?"

Oh, he liked Alki. I have pictures of Peter hugging Alki when he was a baby. And they both liked you a lot when you were a baby. It wasn't until you got older that they were mean to you! They used to tease you so much.

The bassinets we had back then were so flimsy. I think they were made of plastic. We didn't have anything of good quality. We'd stick you right in the car in those bassinets. No car seats, nothing. Now you can't even leave the hospital unless you have a car seat installed correctly.

I started wondering and ask, "Did you get any help from anybody when you had all three kids at home?"

No, not really. I was on my own. Marios was around, but he was young and going to college. Eglie wasn't really helping me. She had her two kids to take care of, your cousins Susie and Peter, plus she was working as a seamstress for the dry cleaners. Lygia was still dropping by with all of her Cypriot friends. I had to entertain them, make them coffee and put out snacks.

Then when you were nine months old, Daddy wasn't happy with the way things were. He didn't like his job anymore. He needed a change. I went along with him. We sold the house, packed everything up, and moved back to Cyprus. I think we gave a few things to Eglie and most of our furniture went to Lygia's basement. And that's when my next journey starts and the real stories begin!

Motherhood, Part 2

Passport photo: Roula with Peter, Irene, and Alki

A SERIES OF MISHAPS AND A "STRICT" MOTHER-IN-LAW

This was in June of 1967. As I said, you were nine months old, Alki was three, and Pete was six. We packed whatever we were taking with us in two big trunks and had them shipped to Cyprus. Then I packed our suitcases and off we went. We first took an airplane from Youngstown to New York.

Mom paused briefly then asked, "I told you about the helicopter ride, right?"

I responded, "You mentioned it briefly the last time we talked. Tell me about it again."

Oh my gosh! When we landed in New York City, we had to go from one airport to another to catch our next flight. Maybe we landed in LaGuardia and had to go to JFK? I'm not exactly sure. Anyways, they put us on a helicopter to transfer us. That was the scariest thing. I was holding you so tight and Daddy was holding your brothers. But we finally made it to Cyprus. We stayed there for six months. Thank goodness your dad took a leave of absence from his job. If he had quit, we would have been OUT OF LUCK!

By the time we got there in 1967, my mom had already been in Australia for four years. She left Cyprus in November of 1963, after my sister Goulla married Giannaki. My mother finally joined my father in Melbourne. She continued to work as a seamstress to make enough money to send my brother, Marios, to attend medical school in St Louis.

When I arrived, my sister had your cousins, Costa and Petros. Petros was born in September of 1966. The two of you are the exact same age. We really didn't have any place else to stay, because everybody was busy with their own families. So, we ended up with my mother-in-law, your YiaYia Susanna, and my father-in-law, your Pappou Petros.

I ask, "Did Dad find a job when you got there?"

No, that's one thing. He couldn't find a job. He was looking and everybody in the family was trying to help him. Your cousin, Petros, just told me, that his father, Giannaki, and your dad, wanted to open up a little grocery store together. It was going to be in the center of town in Larnaca. They call this area, the "Acropolis." However, it never amounted to anything. He told me this after your father died. He commented, "Maybe now they can open up their grocery store together in heaven." I had never heard this story before. So, I said back to him, "I have no idea what you are talking about." I'll have to ask my sister, Goulla, about this next time we talk.

My cousin, Nonni, tried to get him a job too. But it didn't amount to anything. There were no manufacturing plants, like in the United States. Your dad wasn't really a business man. I'm not even sure how much money we brought with us to Cyprus. Your dad was in charge of all of our finances. He took care of everything.

I enrolled Peter in school while we were there. Actually, the principal of the school he went to use to be one of my teachers. He remembered me.

We had fun spending time with all of the relatives and their kids. But you know... YiaYia Susanna was a little "strict." Let's put it this way. She thought I wasn't controlling my kids. She wanted me to be stricter with them. For example, she expected me to put all of you down for a nap during "siesta." Come on, my kids weren't tired in the middle of the afternoon, especially the boys. Besides, we would all wait on the balcony for the ice cream man to come. Why would my kids want to take a nap and miss the ice cream man? Another thing that would make her mad was how the kids in the neighborhood would play and run in and out of each other's houses. She felt as though it was not proper for me to allow my kids to run around the neighborhood and go into other people's houses. Nor did she want the neighbor kids in her house. The lady who lived next door was fine with it. She had all boys and didn't care. You know, the kids had to entertain themselves playing and running around outside. There weren't even any TVs.

So...So...I don't know.

Then, there was this other time. Your father had gone somewhere with Giannaki. Maybe out to his property, the fields where he planted. I was by myself and she started attacking me about how I was raising my kids. I got very upset. Enough already. I put you in your stroller, grabbed the boys, and we left on foot. Of course, where were we going to go? We ended up at my sister's house. Meanwhile, Giannaki dropped your dad off at the house before heading home. Your dad walked in only to find that we weren't there. He asked his mother, "Where are Roula and the kids?" His mother responded, "I don't know. They took off." There were no phones for him to call. But he figured that I was at my sister's house. So, he came and got me.

It must have been a lot for YiaYia Susanna. She had to take care of us. She cooked for us and did our laundry. YiaYia Susanna would spend the whole day doing laundry. I helped in any way that I could. But I wasn't used to doing laundry by hand. My mother never let us do laundry when we were growing up. We would help with hanging the laundry and ironing, never with the hand washing. Plus, I had a washer and dryer back in the United States.

In fact, when I first came to the United States, Eglie had one of those old-fashioned washing machines with the roller. Your cousin Sue should have kept that.

I ask, "What else can you remember about those six months?"
Mom responds, "Hmmm...Let me think."

Your cousins, from your father's side of the family, would come to visit us at the house. They would play in YiaYia Susanna's back yard. Well one day, all of the sudden, I heard somebody crying. I ran out back to find that Michalis and Petros tied your brothers up to a tree! I'll have to ask your brother, Pete, if he remembers this, because he was six years old. They were kids, just playing. All of YiaYia Susanna's grandkids were wild. I don't know why she chose to single out my kids?

"Tell me about Alki almost drowning," I say.

"Yes, twice." Mom laughs and laughs and laughs. "And your brother, Pete, he had the heel of his foot chewed up by the spoke of a bicycle!"

I respond, "Oh, I want to hear about that first."

Your dad was taking the boys on a bicycle ride. He put Alki in front of him, on the bar in the middle, and he put Peter on the little seat behind him. He told the boys to keep their feet spread apart and away from the bike. However, Peter put the heel of his foot in the spokes and it got scraped up really bad. We had to take him to the hospital.

Alki, the first time, almost drowned right in the back yard. YiaYia Susanna had a rain barrel back there that she would use to water her flowers. She loved her flowers so much that she would water them twice a day. So, I made Alki a little paper boat. One day he was playing with his boat in the rain barrel that was filled with water. I had other kids to watch, too. So, I wasn't sitting there staring at him. The next thing I know, I hear him crying. I run towards the barrel, where I find him standing upright inside of it, soaking wet. I think he bent over too far, causing him to go in head first. Good thing he was able to turn himself around and stand himself upright. Otherwise, he could have drowned. You know, they say, that you can drown in just four inches of water? He didn't know what happened because he was only four years old. I found him coughing and crying. He was soaking wet. After that incident, no more paper boats for Alki.

I wonder, "What did my YiaYia Susanna say about that incident? You must have been in big trouble after she found out?"

Mom replies, "Well, maybe she didn't know about it, because I didn't tell her." The second time that he almost drowned was at the beach. A huge wave came and took him under! I actually saw that happen.

Another thing that happened to Alki...again more laughter...The neighbors had this big dog that the kids would play with. It was a friendly dog, I guess, until Alki tried to ride him like a horse. The dog turned around and bit him right over the eyebrow! We took him to the hospital for that. I think they gave him a shot, just in case the dog had rabies or something. He still has a scar from that incident.

Mom comments, "I don't think anything happened to you."
I respond, "Thank goodness."

Let me think for a minute...Was YiaYia Mariannou around during this time? I don't remember going to any other houses from my side of the family, besides my sister's house. Somebody, however, from my side of the family... Maybe it was YiaYia Mariannou. They bought you a potty chair, because you were almost trained by the time you were nine months old. You were a good baby. I would sit you on that potty chair. You ate while sitting on it. Then after you ate, you pooped. Everybody was so surprised. In fact, I brought all of these jars of baby food with me from the United States. But once you tasted that Cypriot food, you wanted nothing to do with them. I ended up giving the jars of baby food to my sister and she fed them to Petros.

Mom continues: Wait a minute. Now I remember. I went to my cousin, Lefteri's, graduation. Yes, his high school graduation. He was an honor student and received a lot of awards. He was a smart one, like your cousin Petros. I took the three of you. Which I shouldn't have done. It was a long ceremony. Your brothers were acting up and Alki had to go to the bathroom. There were no bathrooms because the ceremony was outdoors. I ended up taking him...

So much more laughter from Mom...

Poor Alki. I had your brothers dressed so nice, with long pants and dress shirts. Well, he had to poop. I had to figure out what to do. I took him off to the side. I pulled his pants down and told him to squat down. Well, he lost his balance and fell backwards!

Suddenly, more laughter emerges from Mom. It's so infectious, that I begin to laugh as well.

Then Mom says, "I don't know if I ever told him this story. Next time we get together, we have to tell him all of the things that happened to him when we were in Cyprus."

Now what was I supposed to do? We were in the middle of nowhere. So, we just put him in the car and drove home. You know...the whole car was smelly. That's when YiaYia Susanna really started questioning me. I told her to just get the water hot. I needed to give him a bath and his clothes were...oh you know.

It's funny now, but it wasn't funny then. We had to leave the graduation and Giannaki had to clean his car. But I suppose accidents happen, I guess.

Peter was older. He was more independent and you were a baby. So, we were looking out for you. I guess that left Alki, always getting in to trouble.

And we went to Ayia Napa with my side of the family. Theio Vasso liked to do things with family when he came to Larnaca. Ayia Napa was a nice place to spend the day. We were all together in two cars, Theio Vasso's and Giannaki's. I don't know how we ever fit in two cars. There was a lot of us. We used to pile in. We would put all of the kids on our laps and make it work. We did it often.

Anyways, it was a beautiful day. Half way there, all of the sudden, the sky got really dark and the wind began to blow. Both of the cars stopped, on the side of the rode. We had no idea what was going on, so we started to get out of the cars. All of the sudden, Theio Vasso realized that it was a tornado that came out of nowhere. We were instructed to stay in the cars and close our windows. We could see the funnel blow right past us. All of the sudden, it was gone. It evaporated. I don't remember ever experiencing anything like that in Cyprus. We were able to continue our trip to Ayia Napa. I actually have pictures of us at Ayia Napa from that day.

From left to right: YiaYia Mariannou, Goulla, Theia Eleni, Petros, Giannaki, Androulla, Costa, Irene, Marianna, Alki, Peter, Roula, Demos

The next day, we heard on the news, that the tornado had hit a movie theatre. Luckily there weren't any people in there because it was leveled. We were lucky. It could have picked us up right in our cars and carried us away.

It was getting closer to the six-month mark, and we definitely knew that we weren't going to stay. We didn't have a choice. We had to go back to the United States. Otherwise, you would have all been raised as Cypriots in Cyprus.

My son, Dylan, finally chimes in, "I wouldn't even be here, if you had stayed in Cyprus." I respond, "No you wouldn't, would you?" All three of us ponder for a moment and say in unison, "Nope."

My mom responds, "Your mother would have been married to a Cypriot."

Dylan comments to me, "And you would be warm." I add, "Yup, warm and tan."

Roula continues: Although I always said, if I ever had a daughter, I would never force her into marriage, unless it was with somebody that she chose. I would never arrange a marriage for her. No way! It worked for me, but it wasn't easy.

The Departure

I then ask, "So, you packed up your trunks, in order to have them shipped back to the United States?"

We only took one trunk and all of our suitcases back to the United States. We left one trunk and a lot of stuff behind in Cyprus. Did I tell you about the cat that had babies in one of our suitcases?

I curiously reply, "You did not tell me."

The bedroom that we were staying in was all open. There were no doors or screens on the windows. We had all of our suitcases lined up on the floor. There was nowhere else that we could put our clothes. One day I went in to the bedroom to get some clothes. I looked down and saw all of these baby kittens inside one of the suitcases. They were just born. Ewe. I screamed! Your Pappou Petros came in with a garbage bag. I know, but what were we supposed to do? I didn't know where the mother was. At the time it was just the babies who were just born. They were really slimy. Your YiaYia Susanna had to wash all of the clothes that were in that suitcase. That mother cat found a nice place to have her babies.

Mom shutters, again, "Ewe."

We did a lot of things while we were there for those six months. We visited family and they took us to nice places. Maybe if my mother, your YiaYia Athena, was still in Cyprus, at that time, things would have worked out better for me. But I don't know. She probably would have been living with Goulla. We still wouldn't have had any other place to stay, other than your YiaYia Susanna's house.

So, we packed up and flew back to the United States. No helicopter this time. However, we had to get on a bus when we landed in New York to take us from one terminal to the next. We had to get all of our luggage and go through customs when we first landed. We had five big suitcases, carry-on bags, a diaper bag, plus the three of you to look after. We had everything, because we watched it go underneath the bus, before we got on. We know this for sure. However, when we got to the other terminal, there were only four suitcases. We asked where the other one was. They insisted that there were only four to begin with. We couldn't argue. We were going to miss our next flight. Plus, we had three kids to look after.

They took the best suitcase, one with a hard case. It was your daddy's. It had all of his clothes in it. He came back to the United States with nothing. We never got it back. We tried to put in a claim, but never got anywhere.

Actually, our citizenship papers were in that suitcase, too. They were gone. I'm sure whoever took the suitcase, maybe took the clothes and threw out the papers. Who knows?

Anyways, we made it back to the United States and our life in Youngstown, Ohio, began again...

Mom looks at her watch and notices that it's 5:00 p.m. Realizing that we had been talking for almost an hour straight, she comments, "Oh shoot, we forgot to watch Akis." The three of us had gotten so lost in this conversation that we neglected to watch Mom's favorite Greek cooking show, Kitchen Lab, with chef Akis Petretzikis. Broadcast daily on a Greek Satellite station, not a day goes by that she doesn't mention something that he has made. I have to admit, he's not that bad to look at. In fact, I'm thinking that Mom may even have a little celebrity chef crush on him. I don't blame her one bit. However, we made up for it that evening by having our own little cooking show and indulging in Greek chicken meatballs and lemon butter orzo, for dinner.

The next morning, I decided to call Mom's cellular company to ask about switching her over from her flip-phone to the I-phone. All that was required was removing her SIM card from the old phone and placing it in the new phone. She already had a cellular plan that had unlimited text and talk, in addition to a small amount of data, that she had been paying for and not using. Dylan and I agreed, we would make the switch while we were visiting. We had 24 hours to show her how to use it and answer any questions that may arise.

While Dylan began the process of setting up the phone, I noticed that Mom was pacing the room back and forth. I could tell that she was feeling anxious and she was looking visibly upset. I asked her if she was okay. She looked directly at me and responded adamantly, "You know I don't like change." Dylan and I reassured her that she would be fine. We said, "You are smart and a quick learner. We promise. After trying the I-phone for a while, if you don't like it, we can switch back to your flip phone." She responds, "I don't want text messages to replace getting phone calls. I want people to call me, if they want to talk to me, not text me." I confidently agreed that daily phone calls with friends and family would continue.

Up until this moment, I never thought of my mom as somebody who didn't like change. After all, her whole life did nothing but change, sometimes at a pace so fast, she never even had a chance to catch up. I always thought of my mom as being stubborn, a trait that has, at least to me, magnified, as she has gotten older. However, I now reflect back on a conversation that I was having with a friend a couple of years ago, regarding my mom and her stubborn nature, especially when it came to her not wanting others to care for my father as his health declined. My friend, Kathy, who never met my mom, said, "Your mom isn't stubborn. She's surviving, anyway that she knows how."

I've pondered this comment since then. It's all starting to make sense to me now. My mom has endured with grace and survived situations that would have made many others crumble. So, I now ask myself, hasn't she earned the right to resist change and rest in the comfort of familiarity at this stage in her life?

Coming to America, Again

With the apartment remodel above our garage 95 percent complete and the upcoming 80-degree temps in the forecast, I figured that now would be a great time to have Mom come and stay with us, here in Elma, for a couple of weeks. After all, we could benefit from a little change in our daily routine, including some R&R at our backyard pool, especially after months of being confined to our homes due to the quarantine. Aside from the newly remodeled apartment, we were also excited to show YiaYia the newest member of family, our 12-week-old Cavachon puppy, Declan. Let's just say, it was love at first sight. We quickly discovered that Declan's favorite spot was the shadiness found underneath YiaYia's chair outside in our front yard. It is here that we would resume our conversation about our return to Youngstown, Ohio, after having lived in Cyprus for six months.

We moved back in the winter of 1967/1968. We had to start our lives all over again from the beginning. We rented a small apartment for about a year. Thank goodness your dad was able to go back to work at Youngstown Sheet and Tube. I enrolled Peter in Adam's school. Your brother Peter went to a lot of different schools in a short amount of time. We were finally able to buy a house again in 1969. That's when we moved to Mistletoe Ave. We lived there for a couple of years.

So, let me think about Mistletoe...

Alki, Peter, and Irene

Peter and Alki went to Sheridan school while we lived there. I think you started kindergarten there, but we moved to Boardman halfway through your kindergarten school year. We had those neighbors, remember the school teacher, Maury, and her husband? And we had those Lebanese neighbors. You were friends with their kids, Laurice and Noel. I used to run in to Laurice a lot when she was a pharmacist at Giant Eagle. I haven't seen her in a while. I think she moved recently.

There was an Italian family, too, that had kids. We had some really good neighbors on Mistletoe. Actually, Maury, the school teacher, would help Alki, because he was having some trouble with his speech. Funny thing, later when we moved to Boardman, they also moved to Boardman. We kept in touch. In fact, you babysat for their kids when you were old enough.

In 1969, my brother, Marios, graduated from medical school. I had a big party for him. I invited a lot of people. I had tables and chairs set up in the backyard. But it started raining. So, we had to put everybody inside the enclosed porch that was on the back of the house.

Also, during this time, in 1970, my sister, Goulla, travelled to the United States for a couple of weeks. Back in Cyprus, she took ill. She was having bouts of dizziness that were causing her to be unable to care for her three children. So, our mother left Australia and went back to Cyprus to help her with the kids. In the meantime, Marios married Betsy and moved to Cincinnati, to begin his residency. He convinced Goulla to come to the United States to be seen by one of his medical colleagues.

The trip was appealing to her at the time because our family doctor from Cyprus and his wife would be traveling with her. They would be visiting a son in New York, who was studying to be a doctor. However, once they landed in New York City, their son came to pick them up, leaving Goulla alone, all by herself, in JFK airport. She was supposed to get a connecting flight to Pittsburgh (the closest airport to Youngstown, Ohio) but she didn't know how to go about doing that. Nor did she know or speak the English language very good, either. She was scared to death.

We were at the Pittsburgh airport waiting for her. The first flight from NYC landed and she wasn't on it. Then we waited for the next flight (the last flight of the evening) to land. She wasn't on that one either. We were so worried about her when they told us that there would be no other flights until the next day. Luckily, Lygia got in touch with her brother- and sister-in-law, who lived in NYC. They went to the airport and found Goulla. I don't know how they managed to find her, but they did. Because she couldn't catch a flight until the next day, they took her to their home where she was able to eat and rest. The next day they took her back to the airport, where they changed her flight, upon Marios' request, that took her directly to Cincinnati. She stayed with Marios, until she was given a prognosis and put on medicine that helped her. Eventually she flew back to Cyprus.

Later that same year, my father moved to the United States from Australia.

After 20 Years: An Unexpected Arrival

I curiously ask, "After all of this time, what made your father, my Pappou Petros, decide to come to the United States to live with us?"

Well, my mother, your YiaYia, left Australia and went back to Cyprus to care for Goulla and help with her kids. Although my father had two brothers and a sister living in Australia, he was alone. He must have realized that he was getting older and that he didn't know his children, after all of these years.

Just to be certain I didn't miss anything along the way, I question, "He never returned to Cyprus after he left, when you were eight years old?"

Roula's father Petros back in Cyprus after his time in the United States.

Nope. Never. I hadn't seen him for twenty years. It was a very weird situation. It was all my mom's doing, I guess. She didn't want us to go with him to Australia. He was supposed to go there, make money, and eventually return. But he never did. Then he decided to come to the United States after all this time had gone by. I don't know how old he was when he arrived here. I'll have to check his birth certificate when I get back to Youngstown. However, I'm thinking he must have been in his middle sixties.

My mind is flooded with so many questions, "Had you been in contact with your father, over the years?"

Mom responds, "Oh yes, we would write letters to each other. It's not like we didn't know he existed."

I'm not exactly sure how he got to California from Australia. But I do know that he took a train from California to Youngstown. We waited at the train station in Youngstown for his arrival. I remember going there at midnight. He brought a lot of stuff with him from Australia that we really didn't need. He arrived with two big trunks.

It was weird to see him after all those years. I didn't know him. I had to adjust to the fact that he was my father after all of this time had gone by. There was an extra room (almost like a family room) downstairs that we turned into a bedroom for him. I think he slept on a sleeper sofa. The house on Mistletoe was small and only had two bedrooms upstairs.

Maybe that was one of the reasons we needed to move, too. The house was too small for all of us. But really, the schools were the main reason we moved from Mistletoe Avenue in Youngstown to Ranier Trail in Boardman. It was a better area and you could all go to better schools.

I wonder, "So Pappou adjusted well to life in the United States?"

He adjusted really quick to life in the United States. Oh yes, he loved it here. We had made a lot of friends in Youngstown. So, he got to know all of our friends. He would go visiting to their houses with us all the time. He LOVED to tell stories about life in Australia. NEVER- ENDING stories. OVER and OVER again. But everybody enjoyed having him around and listening to him.

He knew immediately that he couldn't get very far without a car. So, he took it upon himself to get a driver's license. He'd never driven before. Not even in Australia. He took driving lessons, got his license, and eventually bought himself a car. He was a "go-getter" kind of guy. He learned to drive and was traveling all over. He would even take the six-hour drive to Cincinnati to visit Marios.

"I do remember his hunter green Ford Maverick," I reminisce.

Mom responds, "Yes, and I think your brother Pete ended up with that car after he got his driver's license. I got my license late in life, too. It was after I had all three of you and we had moved back from Cyprus. I must have been in my mid to late 20s. Although I couldn't drive very much because we only had one car."

He got a job as a custodian at Woodside Receiving Hospital (for individuals with mental illness). It was a government job. He must have worked there for ten years because he was able to retire with benefits that included good insurance coverage.

He also got involved as a cantor with the local Greek Orthodox churches. He first started in New Castle, Pennsylvania, then he eventually ended up at our church, St. Nicholas. He never missed going to church on Sunday.

And he was painting houses. Mostly exterior but he painted inside, too. I remember him climbing these big ladders when he painted our house on Ranier before we moved in. He was very particular about his jobs and he took his time when doing them.

He was with us in 1971 when we moved to Ranier Trail in Boardman. Peter was in fifth grade and went to Boardman Center Middle School. Alki was in third grade and went to Stadium Drive Elementary. You were in kindergarten and went to Stadium Drive as well.

I remember it well and respond with joy, "We bought the house because it had a Brady Bunch staircase." Mom replies, "Oh, I don't know anything about that. You guys made that up."

By 1971/1972, Goulla had gotten better. So, my mother made plans to come to the United States from Cyprus, to join my father and live here with us also. However, because of the mishap with Goulla in New York City, my father decided to fly to JFK and meet my mom in the airport when she landed. Then they flew back to Pittsburgh together. He didn't want your YiaYia to go through the same ordeal that Goulla went through. Your Pappou was brave.

Your YiaYia and Pappou lived with us for a while. Then they decided to get their own apartment. Their first apartment was across the street from the Boardman Plaza. They got flooded after a big rain because it was a basement unit. That's when they decided to move to the apartments that were being built at the end of Sugartree, the next street over from us. They stayed there until they went back to Cyprus to live in the early 80s.

The house on Ranier has served its purpose for the past fifty years. We always accommodated a lot of out-of-town relatives, in addition to the time that your YiaYia and Pappou lived with us. Over the years, we had a lot of parties at the house, too. I don't know how I ever managed to cook all of that food, especially for your brothers' graduation parties.

Cypriot Cuisine

Koupepia and Pastichio

It takes a little adjusting to learn to cook like a Cypriot. Gilli Davies in The Taste of Cyprus writes, "Cypriots cook with a smile, a shrug, lots of patience, and more than a little tasting. One of the most important words to apply to Cypriot cooking is PERIPOU, which means approximately!" This makes it difficult to share recipes with others who have never stood in a Cypriot kitchen side by side with their mother or YiaYia. For it is these women who pass down, not so much formal recipes, but the techniques needed to master the art of Cypriot cuisine.

KOUPEPIA

Koupepia in the Cypriot language means, "little cigar." More commonly known as "dolmas," in Eastern Mediterranean cooking, stuffed vine leaves, according to Davies, "Demonstrate the essence of Middle Eastern cooking, intricate and time consuming in their preparation but the pride of a good hostess." In Cyprus, the vines may be planted specifically to serve the dual purpose of providing shaded pergolas, in addition to the staple needed to create this delicacy. However, members of my family, who migrated to the U.S. over the years, have looked to other resourceful methods in order to claim their stake in the vined treasure that grows here in the wild. I guess you can refer to it as foraging.

By mid-June, the Elma Village Green, in Elma, New York, is a bountiful host to the vine leaves needed to make koupepia. While the majority of individuals who walk along the north side of the path without even recognizing their importance, a true Cypriot cook, such as my mom, spots them immediately, as if she struck gold. "Look at them all," mom exclaims, "We will come back in a few days. They will be perfect!"

The first step in making koupepia is in the timing of the readiness of the vine leaves. This is a skill that needs to be as precise as the actual preparation. There is a small window of opportunity when the leaves are large, soft, and tender before they become tough and a delicacy for bugs who eat holes through the leaves. Mom was right. Returning with two plastic Wegmans bags in hand, it took us less than a half hour to gather over two hundred leaves. On this particular trip, others on the path paid no attention to what we were doing. However, over the years, this hasn't always been the case.

> Mom chuckles, "There was the time that Eglie and Stavroula almost got arrested in Mill Creek Park! Angie cracks up every time she tells the story."

Although I vaguely remember this story, I curiously ask my cousin Pete for the details, "Tell me about how your mom (my Theia Eglie) and Stavroula (a very close family friend) would pick grape leaves in Mill Creek Park (a huge metro park in Youngstown, Ohio).

> He responds, "My mom and Stavroula would often go together to Mill Creek Park to pick grape leaves. Angie (Stavroula's daughter) and I would hang out together in the back seat of the car. They would drive around until they spotted the grape leaves, then pull over off to the side of the road, so they could still keep an eye on us in the car while they picked. On one particular occasion, Angie and I were playing in the back seat of the car, when we noticed a police car pull up alongside my mom and Stavroula. The police officer asked them

what they were doing. They explained that they were picking grape leaves. He couldn't understand why they would do such a thing and informed them that it was illegal to pick the leaves. He also informed them that they were not permitted to park alongside the road. He officially gave them a warning before leaving. Angie and I were hiding in the back seat of the car during all of this, so embarrassed that our mothers got busted!"

Mom and I arrive home from the park and place the bags of leaves in the refrigerator. Barely a day goes by when mom abruptly gets up and announces that she is going to wash the leaves and cut off any remaining stems in preparation for blanching the leaves and beginning the stuffed grape leaf making process. Although I have made stuffed grape leaves on my own over the years, on this particular occasion, I became my mom's sous chef. Despite my confidence in feeling as though I have mastered some recipes, it never fails, Mom always throws a curveball, adding something or doing something that I was unaware of in my previous attempts at Cypriot cuisine.

We decided that we were going to use two pounds of ground beef in order to make approximately 100 koupepia. This will give us plenty to eat over the next few days with extra to put in the freezer. To the uncooked beef we add 1 cup of raw white rice, one 14 oz. can diced tomatoes, one 8oz. can tomato sauce, 2 tsp. salt, ½ tsp. pepper, a bunch of finely chopped onion, a good amount of freshly chopped parsley, and a smidge of freshly chopped mint. Mom, like any skilled cook, places both of her hands in the mixture and begins to thoroughly combine. Once she is satisfied, she places the bowl aside and washes her hands.

The large pot of water that I have placed on the stove comes to a full boil. Mom places about fifty leaves in the pot to blanch or soften them. A few minutes later she announces, "You know they are ready as soon as they begin to change color and darken a bit." She gives them a quick stir, strains them, and rinses them under cold water to cool them off so that we can begin to handle them. Carrying them over in a big wire colander, we carefully begin reshaping them, hanging some over the edge of the colander and laying others out onto our cutting boards. I quickly learn the importance of having the end, where the stem was, facing toward me and the vein side (back side) of the leaf turned up, to facilitate the stuffing and rolling process.

With Mom and me working on either side of my kitchen island, we placed approximately one rounded teaspoon of meat, give or take depending on the size of the leaf, about 2/3 of the way down from the stem, folded the stem end over the meat, folded the ends in, and continued rolling until a tight little package of mouth-watering delight was created. We repeated the process, blanching more leaves as needed, until all of our meat filling was gone. Looking down at our work, we admired the uniformity of our rows of koupepia nestled together neatly in a single layer and split into two casserole dishes.

At this point, Mom takes over, drizzling the koupepia with olive oil and sprinkling them with lemon juice. She then instructs me to fill each casserole dish with water, about 2/3 of the way up, until the grape leaves are almost, but not completely, covered. This is an important step needed to ensure that the rice in the meat mixture cooks appropriately. Finally, Mom covers the koupepia with the remaining blanched grape leaves, forming a blanket over the top, before covering tightly with aluminum foil. We place them in a preheated 375-degree oven and cook for about one hour and 15 minutes, or until they are hot and steamy and most of the liquid has been absorbed. Of course, Mom and I must each taste one once they come out of the oven. The ease with which one can be popped into your mouth, after slightly cooled, without anyone even noticing, makes it all worthwhile. Another successful day in a Cypriot kitchen.

A few more days go by and we are nearing the end of YiaYia's two-week stay here in Elma. She wishes to go back to the park to pick more grape leaves to take home with her to Youngstown. The following Monday she repeats the whole process, on her own this time and in her own kitchen. As soon as the koupepia are pulled out of the oven, she carefully divides them up into separate containers and begins to call her niece (my cousin Sue), her grandson Alec, and her grandson Nick. She announces, "I've made grape leaves, if you'd like to come and get some." One by one they drive over for a quick visit as they pick up their evening dinner, a delicacy they were not expecting. It goes without saying, YiaYia, like most Cypriot cooks, has held our family together through her love of cooking and the joy that she gets in sharing her food and Cypriot culture with us.

PASTICHIO

When I'm asked to describe "pastichio" to individuals who are unfamiliar with the Greek/Cypriot dish, I often find myself referring to it as "Greek Lasagna." More recently, however, I came across a more suitable comparison for this pasta and meat casserole with cream sauce, termed "pastitso" by the Greeks and "pastichio" by the Cypriots. Perhaps my American friends and family can envision a cross between lasagna and macaroni and cheese. Maybe? Maybe not? Still confused? With my mom's assistance, I will try to clarify a bit further.

Pastichio is a staple in most Greek/Cypriot celebrations and is included as part of the meal at many weddings, festivals, and christenings. For my family, it isn't considered a holiday or birthday celebration unless pastichio is being served. In fact, YiaYia's six grandsons love this dish so much that she will go through the arduous process of preparing pastichio for them on random occasions, just to see the joy in their eyes as she announces, "I made pastichio!" In fact, it is so treasured among YiaYia's grandsons that when Alec was asked by his parents one year what kind of cake he wanted for his birthday, he responded with, "I don't want a cake. I want pastichio!"

Since Mom was staying with us here in Elma for two weeks during the summer of 2020, we had plenty of time to plan and prepare meals together. With over 100 koupepia under our belt, Mom thought it was a good idea to make pastichio next for the family. When making pastichio on my own, I personally consider the whole process to be a chore. However, since I had my mom here to help with the preparation and the clean-up, I decided to go along with her suggestion. On this particular occasion, after having indulged in the layered goodness of our creamy creation for dinner that evening, we all agreed the pastichio was exceptional. Mom proudly commented, "I need to remember exactly what we did this time. It came out perfect."

The following is a re-cap, in my mom's own words, of the exact recipe ingredients and technique used to create our pastichio on this particular day (June 16, 2020).

1. To one pound of cooked penne pasta, mix in a couple tablespoons of butter and a ½ cup of grated parmesan or Romano cheese. Set aside.

2. In a separate pan, sauté one pound of ground beef with onions and fresh chopped parsley. Once brown, add one teaspoon salt, ½ teaspoon pepper, ½ teaspoon cinnamon, one small can of tomato sauce, and 6 oz. of red wine. Allow this to simmer, covered, for about 15 minutes until most of the liquid is absorbed. Set aside.

3. For the bechamel sauce…Over low to medium heat, melt 8 tablespoons of butter in a saucepan (olive oil can be used in place of butter). Whisk in 10 tablespoons of flour. Cook, whisking continuously for several minutes. Slowly add four cups of warmed milk to the flour and butter mixture. Keep whisking for several minutes, until it begins to thicken. At this point, slowly add four beaten eggs to the bechamel sauce, along with one cup of grated parmesan or romano cheese, a little bit of salt, and a dash of nutmeg or cinnamon, to taste.

Now it's time to put everything together

1. We mix the meat with the noodles along with a ladle full of bechamel. Not too much bechamel. You need to make sure you have enough for the top.

2. Pour the entire mixture into the bottom of a greased 9 by 13 baking pan or casserole dish. This ensures that it doesn't fall apart when you cut it and serve it.

3. Top with the bechamel sauce, spreading evenly with a spatula so that it is covered in its entirety and some of the sauce seeps down into and through the noodle mixture. At this point you can refrigerate and bake the next day or even freeze it and bake it later. That's what they do at the church for the festival.

4. Bake in a preheated 350-degree oven for about an hour, until it starts to get golden on top. Allow to cool slightly before cutting and serving.

5. Now it's time for all of the clean-up!

YiaYia cautions, "This is a lot for one person. When I'm doing it by myself, I like to clean up as I go along."

CINNAMON PAXIMADIA

Is it considered stealing a recipe if, while you are assisting someone with baking Greek biscotti (using a recipe created by the person who you are assisting), you memorize the recipe (because the person who you are assisting refuses to share the recipe with you), write the recipe down and share it with your best friend (who then shares it with her daughter)? Just asking for a friend...

It is a few weeks before Christmas 2020 when I begin sifting through my folder in search of my biscotti recipe. I was hoping that I could substitute some of the ingredients, in hopes of making it vegan or at least dairy free. We've discovered over the past year that Tanner has adverse reactions to dairy and I wanted to bake him something that he could eat, guilt free. Rifling through my recipes, many of which are scribbled on scrap sheets of paper, I came across a 5 by 7 sheet of paper that had been ripped out of a notebook with the words "(PAXIMADIA) with cinnamon," written across the top in my mom's handwriting. The recipe followed. There are a few things that I know to be true about this recipe. It is a vegan recipe. I only tried making them once before and they didn't turn out so good. My husband, Brian, absolutely loves them when my mom makes them for him. I quickly scan the recipe and it says 4 to 6 cups of flour? Confused by this, I call my mom for clarification.

She says over the phone, "You know, just add enough flour so that the dough isn't sticky and you can shape it into loaves without too much difficulty."

Without much confidence, we both decide that I should cut the recipe in half, just in case they don't turn out so good. However, to my surprise, the cinnamon paximadia were a hit and I wished that I had made the full recipe. Once cooled, I carefully line a can that used to house Cub Scout caramel corn (similar in size to the large blue Maxwell House coffee cans that my mom uses to store her cookies) with a large Ziploc bag and carefully place the paximadia inside for all to enjoy at their leisure.

It is the week in between Christmas and the New Year when I decide to make a homemade hot chocolate for Brian and me. After we take a sip of the chocolatey goodness, I think that it would pair well with my cinnamon paximadia. I look to the counter and the can is no longer there. Puzzled, I ask Brian, "Where are the biscotti?" He says, "I hid them. You all had enough, and I barely had any!"

During one of our following phone conversations, I tell mom how Brian hid the paximadia. She begins to laugh. I then ask her, "How did you even get this recipe?"

You know Jamie from church? She had her own restaurant, "The Grecian Gourmet." She is an excellent cook and baker. She is the one who created the recipe for cinnamon paximadia. Because they have no eggs or butter in them, they can be eaten during lent or other times, when people are fasting. She began making them and selling them to the parishioners at our church. But that Jamie is SO STINGY with her recipes. She won't give any of them away. Not even her pastichio recipe. So, I'm not exactly sure how, but it was Joanne who got the recipe for the cinnamon paximadia. I think Joanne was at church one day, helping Jamie make them. On the "sly," Joanne wrote down the ingredients. Then she passed it on to me and I wrote it down for you.

Mom is now laughing...

I don't know if Jamie knows that we "stole" her recipe! I don't think that she does. We never told her. They come out good when we make them. I think that they are as good as hers. However, sometimes when I'm lazy, I just order them from Jamie. She made them for your dad's 40-day memorial service.

So that's the story about the cinnamon paximadia...

It is a few days later and I am making dinner for the family. On this particular occasion, I had a bit to juggle in the oven. So, in addition to the upper oven, I decided to preheat and use the lower oven, to complete dinner in a timely fashion. Brian walks in the kitchen and shouts, "What are you doing?" I explain to him my oven dilemma. Panicked and to his dismay, he opens the lower oven and pulls out the can that he had hidden with the remaining cinnamon paximadia, the Ziploc bag had melted and stuck all over his hidden treasure.

*I hesitate to share the recipe for fear of legal repercussions. I would hate for Roula to end up in jail twice in her lifetime!

Koliva

As a child growing up in Youngstown, Ohio, attending St. Nicholas Greek Orthodox church services on Sunday mornings was nothing short of agonizing. Well, at least I am being honest. Adding to my dismay was noticing when there was a small table set up in front of the altar and to the right of the Royal Doors, upon which sat a candle and a tray of Koliva (boiled wheat berries that are mixed with powdered sugar, cinnamon, sesame seeds, slivered almonds, walnuts, golden raisins, and pomegranates). This alerted me to the fact that a Mnimosino (a memorial service that honored the dead) was going to occur at the end of the already two-hour long liturgy. This was an eternity in my eyes. And what dampened my spirits even more was when the memorial service was dedicated to more than one person. At times, several families wished for prayers for their departed and often extended the Mnimosino to family members who had passed anywhere from forty days prior to annually on the anniversary of their death.

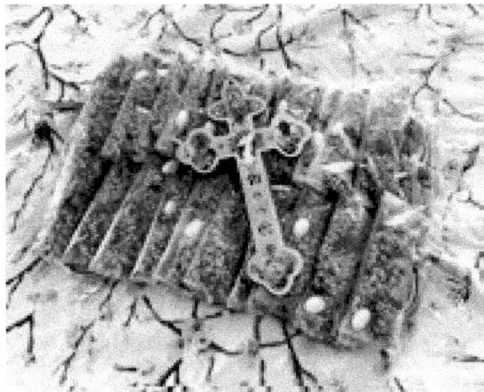

Roula's first time making koliva.

I would sit and listen to the priest listing the names, one by one, as the chains of the incense-filled chalice moved rhythmically back and forth over the tray of koliva. It wasn't until the priest began his chanting of "Eonia I Mnimi" that I knew the service was closing in on the end. In fact, I often found myself repeating the hymn internally, despite not knowing what I was chanting or humming from deep within. Perhaps I was celebrating the close of the church service. Perhaps the repetitive nature of the song sung in Greek three times, brought a strange sense of calm and peace over me. One of the only redeeming factors to all of this was afterwards, when we were able to indulge in the individually wrapped bags of Koliva, that were placed on a table in the church's social hall. Here, parishioners participated in a social gathering that on most Sundays, included coffee and doughnuts.

In October of 2019, it was my family's turn to honor the 40-day passing of my father's death. Mom says to me over the phone a couple of weeks prior to the service, "I'm going to have Helen Mays make the Koliva for your father's Mnimosino. I called her and she immediately told me that she charges $100. I'm willing to pay her whatever she wants. I didn't even ask her. I'm not sure why she said that? Oh, and I'm going to also serve feta cheese and olives along with some koulourakia (Greek twisted cookies) during the coffee hour after church." I happily agreed with whatever my mom wished for on what I knew would be a very important and emotional day. However, at 53 years old, I had no idea as to the significance of Koliva and a 40-day Mnimosino. So, I took it upon myself to do a little research.

The Greek Orthodox faith is steeped in rituals that hold symbolic meaning. The traditional memorial or Mnimosino, takes place forty days after death. It is believed by the Greek Orthodox Church, that the soul of the departed wanders here on earth for forty days following their death, visiting their homes and even their graves, before departing this world and reuniting with their bodies and with Christ. Individuals who follow the Eastern Orthodox tradition believe in resurrection and everlasting life through Christ after death. The offering of Koliva at this service is in memory of the dearly departed. It is symbolic of death and resurrection. The wheat berries represent the hope for everlasting life.

Knowing this and experiencing my own father's Mnimosino, made this ritual sweeter for me since experiencing it as a child more than forty years ago. I was attentive when the priest began to chant "Eonia I Mnimi," first in Greek and then switching to English, "May his memory be eternal." Once again, I find myself chanting these words, even out loud at times, when nobody is home. It has more power behind it and the same feeling of calm and beauty overwhelms me.

As the one-year anniversary of my father's passing, August 22, 2020, rapidly approaches, Mom begins to mentally prepare for the one-year Mnimosino that will take place on Sunday the 23rd. I am on the phone with her when she states, *"You know, I think I'm going to try and make the koliva this time. I didn't like Helen Mays' attitude when she told me that she charged one hundred bucks. I think I saw Akis making it on his cooking show. Maybe you can look up the recipe for me?"* A week or so later I oblige with this request and read the ingredients and steps to my mom over the phone. She says, *"I think I'm going to try and make just a little bit, first, in order to see how it comes out before I make enough for forty or fifty people."*

Over the course of the next several days, Mom gathers up the ingredients at "Rulli Bros." grocery store and "Ghossain's" Middle Eastern bakery. She begins the process of soaking the wheat berries the night before, boiling them the next morning, and laying them out to dry for several hours before mixing in the rest of the ingredients. She calls me later that day. *"I think it was a success, for the most part. I gave some to your cousin Sue, the Cypriot that lives down the street from me, and I even let my neighbor, the mail lady Susie, try it. They all really liked it. Then I drove some over to Bill and Joanne's house. They also liked it; however, Vasilis (Bill) suggested I cook the wheat a little bit longer, because he thought it was just a little hard."*

I arrive in Youngstown on the Thursday prior to the Mnimosino. By Saturday the 22nd, Mom is feeling anxious. I ask, "Do you want to take a ride over to the cemetery?" She quickly responds, "Yes." I see her grabbing a bag from 'Michael's' craft store. In it are some synthetic flowers. Forest Lawn Cemetery does not permit real flowers to be placed in the vase near Dad's headstone. Mom has been switching them out seasonally over the past year.

She says to me, "Last time I went there, they threw my flowers out! I need to call and find out how often they do that so I can go and get them before they just throw them out." Again, I am supportive of Mom's concerns as we head a couple of miles down Glenwood Avenue to the cemetery. I notice that grass has now grown nicely over the grave that rests beneath a tree. Dad's headstone is abnormally shiny. Mom proudly uses her own scissors to trim the grass around it, and furniture polish to make it shiny." As Mom carefully removes the summer arrangement of yellow and orange flowers, she replaces them with the purple ones in the bag to commemorate the one-year anniversary of Dad's passing. We are all set for tomorrow where, as a family, we will come back after church and sprinkle Dad's grave with the blessed koliva that represents rebirth and eternal life.

Demos on one of his memorable trips back to Cyprus.

By the time I wake up Sunday morning, Mom has "mise en place." She has cooked the wheat berries to perfection, toasted the nuts and seeds, and measured out all of the ingredients into bowls. My son, Dylan, who drove in from Cleveland the night before, my mom, and me are ready to mix the ingredients, portion the koliva into small plastic bags, and place them on the silver tray that mom has pulled out for this special occasion. Mom carefully places a cross on top of the koliva before covering the tray with foil to transport it to church, where it will be placed carefully on the table in front of the altar and to the right of the Royal Doors.

After mass, as friends and family gather in the church hall, wearing their masks of course, due to Covid-19, Mom proudly mentions to the parishioners that she was the one who made the koliva. They nod their heads and their eyes light up in acknowledgement of Roula's culinary skills, as they casually reach for a second bag. As Helen Mays walks by, I see Mom's arm reach out to stop her. At this point I hear mom say, "Helen, I made the koliva myself this time. However, you're the expert. You must taste it and let me know how I did." After some idle small talk, Helen makes her way through the church social hall. Mom casually turns to me with a twinkle in her eye and what I could tell was a smirk under her mask, "I had to say that to her. I didn't want her to feel bad and think that I paid somebody else the $100 bucks to make it!"

ADDENDUM: LATE SEPTEMBER 2020

Approximately one month after my father's Mnimosino, I disclose to Mom that I wrote this story and read it to my writing group on Thursday 9/24. "Oh, did I tell you," she says, "I was at church on Sunday and Helen told me that my Koliva was good? Then Antoinette speaks up and says, 'It was very good!' But then Helen told me that she doesn't put parsley in her Koliva. Her recipe doesn't call for it. I guess she had to find fault with something..."

A Little Comfort
In The Face Of Adversity

It's been quite some time since I had an official interview with Mom. On one of our daily phone chats, I express to her the need to pick up where we left off with her storytelling. She asks, "What do you want to talk about?" I respond, "I was thinking, we could discuss some of our holiday traditions, starting with Halloween. You always made us the best costumes. Or we can talk about the years you worked at the school in the cafeteria and as an aide on the school bus for children with special needs."

Mom ponders for a moment and replies, "I was thinking that we should talk about how your father and I hosted all of the friends and family that came from over-seas to attend university here in the United States."

As I place my phone on speaker and set my iPad to record, I announce, "What a great idea." Mom then states, "I wonder if I should put my phone on speaker, as well? You know, I get tired sometimes, from holding it for so long when we have these conversations." Before starting, I encourage her to do so.

MARIOS PANAYIDES

This is how I want to start, by explaining that there were no universities back home in Cyprus. So, unless the kids wanted to work at a bank or at a store once they graduated from high school, they had to leave Cyprus to attend a university. Some kids would travel to England or to Athens to study. Because I lived here already, my brother Marios had the opportunity to come to the United States. In 1962 after he graduated from high school, Marios wanted to become a doctor. He was accepted for his undergraduate studies at Youngstown University. The name of the school was eventually changed to Youngstown State University. However, when Marios went there it was called Youngstown University. When he arrived, we helped him out by letting him stay with us at our house on Dewey Avenue. In addition to providing him with things that he needed like food and rides to places, we helped him with the American language and customs.

He would take the bus to get to campus. In no time at all he met other international students from Greece and even Cyprus. He adjusted really well. After three years he was accepted into medical school in St. Louis, Missouri. Several of his friends that he met in Youngstown also went to St. Louis to attend medical school. While he was there, he would often catch rides part-way back to Youngstown. Your father would often go and pick him up at different locations and drive him the rest of the way here for a visit. Then your father would take him back. Your father surprisingly never complained. He was always willing to help out in any way he could.

Then of course, we went to Marios' graduation from medical school in 1969. We left the three of you with Theia Lygia for a few days and your father and

I took the bus to St. Louis. It was a long trip but I wanted to be there for my brother. He had no other family in the United States. In the meantime, Marios met Betsy, his first wife, while working at the hospital. She was a nurse at the same hospital. By the time we got to St. Louis for his graduation, we found out that he had already gotten married to her without telling us. Of course, when our mom, your YiaYia Athena found out, she wasn't very happy about it.

But before we found out about his marriage to Betsy something interesting happened. When we first arrived at the bus station in St. Louis, Marios had plans to pick us up and take us to our hotel. However, when we arrived, he wasn't there and we had no way to contact him. You know, it wasn't as easy back then to keep in contact with people. There were no cell phones. So, we just had to wait it out. Eventually he showed up and explained that Betsy's grandfather, who lived in Indiana, was dying. They had to go there to see him. And the funny thing is, her grandfather, who was actually part Greek, started to speak in Greek during the last few moments of his life. Nobody in the family could understand him because they'd never heard him speak anything but English. Luckily Marios was there and he was able to translate for him.

Mom pauses for a moment and says to me, "You never heard this story before?" I respond, "I feel like I have from Uncle Marios at some point in time. It does sound familiar."

Anyways, after the graduation Marios and Betsy were heading to Cincinnati, Ohio so that Marios could begin his residency there. So, your father and I were able to catch a ride with them. But first we stopped in Indiana. Here we met Betsy's family and stayed at their lake house. We then continued on to Cincinnati and eventually took the bus the rest of the way home to Youngstown.

Everyone was very proud of Marios' accomplishment in becoming a doctor. However, your YiaYia Athena and Pappou Petros really had to sacrifice. That's for sure. They needed to continually send him money for school. As a result, my mother ended up moving to Australia to work. While my father was still a painter there, my mother worked in a tomato canning factory. By the time she got to the United States, she never wanted to eat anything that came out of a can.

So that's Marios' story...

LEFTERI PAPAKYRIACOU

In 1975, my first cousin Lefteri, came here to study on a Fulbright Scholarship. He was another smart one from my side of the family. He came to attend one of the universities in Pittsburgh, Pennsylvania. I'm having trouble remembering which one, however. The problem with him was that he had just gotten married to Eva. So, as soon as he arrived, he became very sad, because he had to leave her back home in Cyprus. As a result, he didn't last too long in the United States. I think it was only a few months. At the most, one semester.

Mom pauses, "Yup...Yup..."

He threw it all away because he wanted to be with his wife. He didn't like it here in the United States. Plus, he didn't want to have to stay here during the winter. He became depressed and once he made up his mind, that was that. So, he lost his scholarship and his opportunity to earn his degree and to get a better paying job once he returned to Cyprus.

We tried to help him out as much as we could. We encouraged him to bring Eva here to stay with us. Then he could travel to Youngstown from Pittsburgh on the weekends and see her. We even suggested he rent a small apartment for the two of them in Pittsburgh so that they could be together. We did everything we could to make him happy. We drove back and forth so many times and brought him here. But in the end, because he was homesick, he left and went back to Cyprus.

So anyways, that's Lefteri's story...

ANDREAS ANDREOU

His name was actually Andreas Andreou, but we called him Andrew. He was my mother's cousin Irene's son. Irene was cousin Nonis' sister. She was actually born in the United States but lived in South Africa. Because Irene was a United States citizen, it made it easier for Andrew to come here from South Africa to study.

Nonis and Irene's father was my YiaYia Mariannou's brother. His name was Engrafis. He had a very unusual name. In Greek it means registration. I'm not sure why he was given that name. He married a lady that wasn't Greek or Cypriot. I can't remember her nationality, but I know that she was Catholic.

Anyways, Andrew flew into the Pittsburgh airport. We went to pick him up and we didn't even know what he looked like. We found him wandering around the airport looking lost. I finally approached him and asked him in Greek if he was Andreas. We brought him to our house to stay for a few days before he left for Springfield, Ohio. I believe he was going to study pre-law at Wittenberg University. He ended up going to law school near there and eventually became an attorney in Columbus. He was close to your Uncle Marios, who was a Doctor in Springfield for many years.

Mom pauses, "Marios would probably know more of the details. You might want to ask him."

While Andrew was studying here his father came from South Africa to visit. He's the one that brought us the clock that is shaped like Africa. With the animals on it. It's still hanging in the family room. He also brought us the carved elephant tusk. Eventually Andrew's father died and his mother, Irene, ended up moving back to Cyprus. She lived in Limassol, close to her brother Nonis. She came here to visit us, too.

Mom asks, "Do you remember when Marios drove Irene here from Springfield? It was Christmas time. I have a picture of her standing by our Christmas tree. She stayed with us for a few days. Then when your dad and I went to Cyprus, we got together with her a couple of times."

Andrew did okay for himself. I think he's still a practicing attorney in Columbus, Ohio. Marios keeps in touch with him.

However, he never did get married...

PETROS HADJICOSTA

Then we move on to your cousin, Petros. He was the same age as you. However, before he could leave the country of Cyprus to study at a university, it was made mandatory that all males had to serve in the Cypriot Army for two years, after graduating from high school. He was so smart. All he did was study. While attending school in Cyprus, he would participate in academic competitions throughout Cyprus. If I remember correctly, he even went to Athens, Greece to compete. He was the "top dog" in mathematics. So, it was no surprise that he was given a scholarship to study abroad. However, there was a stipulation attached to it. Once he received his degree, he had to return to Cyprus as a professor and teach at the university there. You see by then, Cyprus had their own university.

So, around 1986 or 1987 he was accepted for his undergraduate studies at Carnegie Mellon University in Pittsburgh, Pennsylvania. He ended up staying there for many years and eventually earned his doctorate degree in statistics from there.

He was a pistol, that one. I don't think that he liked anything about the United States when he first got here. He didn't like the food or the weather. He disagreed with university professors. He even argued with them that they were incorrect in their teachings. Over the years, he's gotten himself into trouble because he was so opinionated. For as smart as he was, he was something else. However, he wanted to be someone. So he stuck with it.

This is a funny story. He didn't know how to wash his own clothes. The first time he tried to do laundry, he put his dirty clothes in the dryer instead of the washing machine. He had a hard time because, as I mentioned before, all he did was study back home in Cyprus. My sister, Goulla, did everything for him. His mother even packed his bags that he brought to the United States. He couldn't find anything once he got here. So, he used to call his mother in Cyprus to ask her where she had packed certain things.

We used to drive back and forth to Pittsburgh and bring him here to Youngstown for the holidays. He was also a daredevil. While he was here your father took him skydiving three times. Your father would do anything for Petros. To this day Petros still acknowledges how much his Theio Demos did for him. He often comments when I talk to him, "Theio Demos never said 'no' to me."

When Petros left Pittsburgh, he moved close to Rochester, New York, and became a statistics professor at Brockport University. Then he left and went to Texas A&M. After that he ended up in New Zealand. Then he took a brief hiatus from teaching and finally returned back to Cyprus after many years. He's currently a professor at a university in Las Vegas, Nevada. He somehow got out of his obligation to teach at the university in Cyprus. I'm not sure how he got away with that, but I know that he wasn't permitted back in the country for quite some time. I'll have to ask him some questions the next time he calls me. I'll let you know what he says.

There is a moment of silence when I interject, "So that's it then? That's everybody, right?"

Mom thinks for a moment, "Yes. It was easier for all of them because your dad and I were here and were able to help them out when they first arrived to the United States. They slept here. They ate here...

Oh wait, we didn't talk about Stella. She wasn't even our relative, but her family was good friends with my cousin Marianna, back in Cyprus."

STELLA

Yes, we need to talk about Stella. She was fun and such a nice girl. When my cousin Marianna from Cyprus found out that her friend's daughter, Stella, would be attending Youngstown State University, she immediately wrote to me and asked if I could contact Stella. In Marianna's letter, she expressed Stella's parents concern about their daughter traveling to a foreign country.

I was willing to help in any way that I could. So, I contacted her at the university because Marianna forwarded me her phone number. When I called Stella, she sounded so happy. We drove downtown and picked her up from her dorm room and brought her here to our house.

She spent a lot of holidays with us. She came here for Thanksgiving and Christmas. I even took her to St. John's Greek Orthodox Church for Easter one year. She brought one of her friends who was dark skinned. I'm not sure what country she was from, but she wanted to take communion. I had to tell her that I didn't think it was a good idea. I think she may have been Catholic. But I know that she wasn't Greek Orthodox.

Stella was in a bad car accident with some friends. I ended up taking her to see Angela Mikulka, the attorney that goes to our church. We also took her to see a skin doctor because she needed plastic surgery. I think she may have ended up getting some money from that accident.

After she graduated from Youngstown State University, she went to Kansas City, Missouri to further her education. She eventually went back to Cyprus and became a professor of English language at the university there. When your dad and I visited Cyprus, her parents and grandmother were so appreciative of our hospitality. They wanted to reciprocate by having us over to their house in Nicosia. They cooked so much food for us.

She called me from Cyprus when she heard about your dad dying. She found out from Marianna and immediately called me. We had a nice chat. She is married now and has a little boy. She is a good person from a good family.

After a few moments of silence, mom says, "Yup, that's it. Do you have enough for a while?" I giggle and respond, "Yes, I have plenty. I'm going to be writing for hours."

The Hot-Lunch Bunch

One of the fondest memories that I had, while attending Board-
man Center Middle School, was being able to see my mom every day
at lunch. If you ask my oldest brother, Pete, I'm sure he would have
a different response.

You were all in school full-time when I started working in 1974. It was the
first job that I ever had. I think that you must have been in first grade, Alki was
in fourth, and Pete was in sixth grade. Pete was already in the Middle School.
I first heard about the job when I went to a PTA (Parent Teachers Association)
meeting at Stadium Drive Elementary School. I met my friend, Regina Burns,
there. She was the one who initially came up to me and started talking about
her job as a cafeteria lady at the Middle School. She told me how much she
enjoyed working there because the hours allowed her to be home when her
kids were home. So, Regina put the idea in my head first and encouraged me
to apply.

Shortly after, we got invited to our neighbor, Buddy Gosh's, engagement
party. While I was there, I was introduced to his fiancé's mother, Mrs. Peters.
Well, she happened to be the manager of the Middle School cafeteria. So, I
expressed my interest in a part-time job. She told me to stop in and fill out an
application, assuring me that she would take care of securing me a position.
At first, she brought me in as a sub, because there weren't any permanent
positions open. However, she would call me to come in quite often. The High
School manager also heard about me and called me to sub there a few times.
But I didn't like working at the High School as much. Finally, when a permanent position opened up at the Middle School, I got the job.

So, I started working for Mrs. Peters. At first it was one and a half hours a day and then it eventually turned into two hours a day. I would work from 11:00 a.m. to 1:00 p.m. Monday through Friday. My primary job was to help set up the line, serve grades five thru eight, and clean up after each lunch period. It was constant. There were quite a few of us working. The only full-time ladies were the manager, the cook, and the baker. They would go in early and start preparing the food that was to be served for the day. We would come in as support: servers, cashiers, set-up, and clean-up. Once I had many years of experience, I would fill in for the cook and sometimes the baker. I really enjoyed baking, not so much the cooking, especially having to handle those big pots of spaghetti and sauce. One thing that I never wanted to do was be a cashier. I didn't feel comfortable handling the money.

I interrupt, "Tell me about the food that you would serve. I remember it being pretty good."

Oh yes. Besides the pizza that we would order from local pizza shops, we would make spaghetti with homemade meat sauce, baked chicken with mashed potatoes and vegetables, and your brother Pete's favorite was ground beef mixed with gravy and served over mashed potatoes. We used to bake and serve real turkeys for Thanksgiving and Christmas. We made our own salad dressings and the grilled cheese was really good. We would dip the bread in melted butter.

It was nice to get out of the house, work with good people, and see all of the kids. We had a lot of fun working together, especially before the kids arrived and after when we were cleaning up. Mary B. was really funny. She would make our manager, Barbara Briggs, who took over after Mrs. Peters left, laugh so hard, that she would pee her pants. Sometimes we would sit and eat together at the end of the day.

We gave ourselves the name, "The hot lunch bunch." We even had t-shirts made that we wore with our white pants. I even sewed my own aprons. Albina Minko, who we called, Bini, was German. We had an Italian lady, named Olga, whose accent was worse than mine, and a Lebanese lady whose name was Ann. And of course, I was Greek. We had a good representation of really nice people working together. We used to go out to dinner together for birthdays and holidays. It was nice to sit and relax...be normal. It was enjoyable having somebody else serve us for a change.

As I mentioned earlier, when I first started the job in the cafeteria, your brother Pete was in Middle School. All of his friends liked to come through my line, because they knew I was going to give them a little extra food, spaghetti or mashed potatoes. We weren't allowed, but if I saw them coming, I'd sneak a little extra onto their plate. Your brother, however, wouldn't even say "hi" to me. He would go into the other line. I told him that he was missing out on extra food, by not coming through my line, but he didn't care. Alki would come through my line once he got to Middle School, along with all of his friends. They were all friendly greeting me with, "Hi Mrs. Santamas," as they went through the line. And of course, you loved having me there. You would even come into the back just to say "hi" to me.

Many of the kids we served never even ate their lunch. The rule was, they had to take everything that was being served in the line. They would swirl their food around on their trays then bring them to us, all yucky, at the end of the lunch period. So much food was wasted. And you know, we had all the condiments and salad dressings on a table towards the front. The kids would make a mess of that. We'd have to clean it, along with all of the tables, after each lunch period. We really had to hustle. It was go, go, go and quite hard at times. We never had time to rest. It's probably how I got Carpal Tunnel, having to handle those big heavy pots and pans. My hands still hurt. We'd even burn ourselves at times, from having to handle hot pans out of the ovens and to our lines. It was intense, but I had fun doing it.

A lot of the kids were wearing retainers back then. Of course, they would take them out and wrap them in a napkin, while they ate. They would forget and dump their tray, along with their retainer into the garbage. Once they remembered, they would panic, because they knew they were going to get in trouble at home for losing their retainers. We would hand the kids rubber gloves and make them dig through the garbage. We weren't about to do it. Some retainers were found. Some were not.

I have to tell you about this one "cheap" teacher, who was in charge of the cafeteria during lunch. I won't mention his name, but he was so cheap. He would go around to the tables and ask the kids, "Are you going to eat your salad? No? Ok then. I'll take it." He was scrounging off of the kids lunches instead of buying his own. He was so cheap. When he did go through the line to buy his lunch he would stand there and count his change.

Most of the teachers, however, were really nice. They had their own lunch room. We would keep it clean for them and make them fresh coffee. They were very appreciative. Sometimes I would bake cookies and bring them in for the teachers and the other lunch ladies. Several of them actually placed orders and bought them from me. One of the ladies from the cafeteria liked my kolache. Of course, my twisted cookies and baklava were always a hit.

I lasted through about four or five managers. After Barbara Briggs left, Jeanie Hagen became my manager and then MaryJane Green. Even though I enjoyed the others, MaryJane was my absolute favorite. She had a big house with a pool. She would invite us over to celebrate the end of the year. Her husband would make us hamburgers and hotdogs. We'd have a great time. She'd also have us over around Christmas. She had the biggest Christmas tree that I had ever seen. The last manager, I didn't care for. When she started, she brought in all of her own people from another school. They would sit around and talk, while I was working so hard to set everything up. After a while I said, "Enough is enough. I'm not doing this anymore." I knew it was time to go. I hung on to this job in order to help pay for your wedding in 1996. However, a year or two later, I quit my job in the cafeteria and focused solely on being an aide on the handicapped school bus.

A Kind and Caring Soul for Those with Special Needs

By the time I left the cafeteria, I had been working on the bus for about ten years. I worked both jobs from 1987-1997. I know that I started the job on the bus in 1987 because that is the year that my mom, your YiaYia Athena, passed away. I went to Cyprus and started my new position a little bit after the school year had begun.

> *Mom reflects for a moment, "I have so many stories that I'm thinking about. I don't know how much you want to write?" I respond, "Tell me as much as you want and if I need to break it up into two parts, I will." She replies, "I was going to start off by telling you the story of how I got my job as an aide on the special-needs bus. Is that, okay?" I am intrigued and reply, "Yes, that sounds great. I do not believe that I know this story."*

Before 1987 they had buses for kids with special needs, but there were no aides on the buses to assist the drivers. My first bus driver, Cindy, used to do everything by herself; drive the bus, operate the lift, and keep her eyes on the kids. She eventually got fed up and went to the supervisor, requesting help. So that is when they posted the position. I wouldn't have known about the position, but I lucked out again, like I did with my job in the cafeteria. Remember our neighbor, Barbara Kinney? Well, she was a secretary at the Middle School at the time. She found out that they were posting jobs for aides on the buses for kids with special needs. So, she approached me and encouraged me to apply. But she cautioned me, "Don't apply for bus 53. Apply for bus 54." You see, bus 53 was the bus that catered to kids with behavioral issues. So, I applied for bus 54 and got the job. I was one of the first people to have the position as aide. There was another lady who went and applied after me. She got bus 53 and wasn't too happy about it. But it didn't matter because, eventually the kids were no longer separated. They were mixed on the two buses according to routes.

Mom interjects, "So, you didn't know this story?" I answer, "No, I had no idea how you got the job as school bus aide."

Because the job on the bus would be four hours per day, it gave me full benefits. I didn't get benefits working only two hours a day in the cafeteria. I put in a full day working both jobs. I would work on the bus from 6:30 to 8:30 in the morning. I would get home by 9:00 a.m., do all of my chores, and head to the cafeteria to work from 11:00 to 1:30. Then back on the bus from 2:00 to 4:00 in the afternoon. I was running from one place to the next. Working two jobs and taking care of things at home was a lot. But I was available to all of you when you needed me. I had the holidays off and the summers. And because everything was so close, it was very convenient for me.

My job on the bus included operating the lift for kids with wheelchairs, but it went beyond that. I had to keep an eye on all of the kids and keep them entertained. We had all kinds of kids on the bus; those with Down Syndrome, Autism, some behavioral (not too many), two girls that were deaf, and even one boy who had Spina Bifida. Then of course there were the kids in the wheel-chairs.

Now I'm going to tell you a little bit more about the kids. I'm going to start with the two little girls who were deaf. The first day we went to pick them up, the mother was frantic. Can you imagine, having to put your two little girls, ages three and five, on a bus? She came and talked to me, "Please take care of my girls." I assured her that I would be good to them and she was not to worry. Their names were Jennifer and Elizabeth. They were so cute. The one would bring her pillow and blanket. Little Elizabeth, who was three at the time, would sneak her pacifier on the bus. Eventually, their mom became very thankful and appreciative once she realized how well I was caring for them. Elizabeth went on to play basketball in high school. Both of the girls ended up getting cochlear implants. Their parents went above and beyond in order to help them acclimate with the other kids.

I ask, "How did you communicate with them?

Actually, Cindy and I went and took an adult sign language course at the high school. But they also read lips. We had no problem communicating with them. We had them on our bus from elementary to middle school. Once they got to high school, they rode the regular bus. Their mother always gave us nice gifts. She even wrote me a letter showing her appreciation. I showed it to my boss. To this day, I run into their mother and she tells me how well they are doing. They both graduated high school, went on to finish college, and eventually got married and had kids of their own.

Then there was the boy with Spina Bifida. He was the happiest boy. You'd never know that he suffered from so many problems. The first time we went to pick him up, his mother was walking alongside him, carrying a small piece of luggage. I inquired about it. She explained to me that he needed everything in the luggage to help him get through his day at school. She assured me that the school nurse would be waiting for him once we arrived. Not only did he walk with crutches, he had a tracheotomy, and a feeding tube. But like I said, he was the happiest boy. He loved to dance. In fact, one day at school, they had a party. He danced so much that he got blisters on the bottom of his feet. You see, he couldn't feel any pain in his legs or his feet so the teachers had to be careful after that and keep a close eye on him. When he graduated from high school, we went to his graduation. He ended up working with computers at a place that catered to kids with special needs. The last time I ran into his mother, she told me how much he loved his job. You know, nothing stopped that boy. Nothing. His name was Kevin. I will never forget him.

And then, of course, we had the kids with Autism. They didn't like loud noises. For example, if there was an emergency vehicle going by, they would cover their ears with their hands and scream. So, if the bus driver and I heard sirens approaching, we would start to sing really loud and clap our hands, in order to distract them. One of the boys with Autism was named Anthony. He was really smart and could spell anything. He was the best. Many of the kids with Autism loved to run. The minute they got off of the bus, they would immediately start running so I had to watch them very carefully.

Let me tell you about "runner boy," Nikki. You know, most of the kids had two parents. However, the stress of raising a child with special needs caused divorces in some of the families. Often, fathers would leave and the mothers would have to take on most of the responsibility themselves. So, Nikki's parents were divorced. His father, however, was very nice. He was often there to greet Nikki when we dropped him off. He would then take him to his home in Campbell, Ohio, after school. As a result of going back and forth between the two houses, Nikki became very familiar with the route from his mother's house on Maple in Boardman to his father's house in Campbell, approximately twenty minutes away. One day we heard on our bus radio that there was a boy missing. He was described as having Autism and being a "runner." We knew immediately who it was. He was eventually found running all the way to his father's house. Luckily, he was okay. I'm not sure how he escaped, but he must have jumped out of a window because after that incident, there were bars placed on the windows of the house.

The kids with Down Syndrome were very loveable. They loved to hug, kiss, and be touched, unlike the kids with Autism, who didn't like it when you touched them. Gina was one of my favorites. She was something else. She stood out because she was one of the few girls with Down Syndrome. Mostly they were boys.

Besides taking the kids to school, we would take them on field trips. Twice a week, as part of a special program for kids with special needs, we would take them either to the grocery store, where they would learn how to shop, or to a restaurant, where they would learn how to order their own meal and eat when out in public. Some kids would go to a workshop where they would learn skills that would help them get a job when they graduated. It was fun going with them on these trips during the day once I left the cafeteria.

Where else would we go? Let me think...Oh, we would do seasonal things, like go apple picking or to the pumpkin farm. The kids really enjoyed going places. The teachers always invited us to go along with the kids. I didn't have to join them. I could have sat on the bus, waited for them, and read, like some of the others used to do. But I always went along and helped the teachers and classroom aides with the kids. They really appreciated it. Oh, and we would take them downtown to the theatre, the Youngstown Playhouse and Powers Auditorium, to see Christmas productions. We'd even go to a food pantry, where the kids would assist in separating the bulk food by weight or quantity into smaller bags. These bags would be distributed to families in need. In fact, we went to the food pantry quite often.

Then of course in 1994, your dad got a job as an aide on another bus. There were more buses that catered to kids with special needs as more kids came into the Boardman school system. Your dad really enjoyed his job also. He worked as an aide for sixteen years.

I went through quite a few bus drivers in my twenty-seven years as an aide. I think a total of five. Cindy was my first driver. She was very competent and knew what she was doing. Cindy eventually left to become a nurse. Then I had a sub named Karen for a short period of time. She was nice. Then they put the bus up for bid and that's when Barbara Moff got the bus. I was with her for fifteen years. We had a good time together. When Barb retired, I had Marj for two or three years. For some reason, nobody liked her. The others felt sorry for me. But I was fine with Marj. I don't know what their issues were with her. When Marj retired, I got Diane. We were together for seven years, until I retired. I really lucked out that I always got along with my bus drivers.

Some of the kids would get tired and stubborn by the end of the day. One afternoon, all of the kids got on the bus, except for Joey. We were waiting for him, wondering where he was? All of the sudden, we see two teachers carrying him towards the bus, one had his arms and the other had his legs. I thought to myself, "Oh boy! We're going to have fun getting him home." But I would talk to him and work on calming him down. One time he took off his shoe and threw it at the bus driver! I swear, some days I needed ten sets of eyes and ten arms to keep everyone under control.

One time, Joey got on the bus with his shoes wrapped in duct tape. You see, there was this classroom aide who I never cared for. She taped his shoes because she couldn't get him to stop taking off his shoes at school. She was so mean. Come on, that wasn't the right thing to do. We took him home to his grandma, who had a really hard time getting his shoes off. She called the school to complain. That never happened again.

Mom pauses, "Let's see what else I have to tell you. I wrote some notes down..."

We didn't have too many kids with behavioral issues. We lucked out. However, one time we had this boy who was very scary. We didn't like the look in his eyes. He ended up getting expelled from school for attacking a teacher. Yup, he actually broke her glasses. I don't know where he went after that, but he didn't last at Boardman for very long.

I got bit a couple of times. And this other girl, who wore a helmet, bashed her head into me with her helmet on. That wasn't fun.

Most of the kids made out pretty good, considering. You know they got jobs after high school. I would run into them at the mall or at the grocery store with their parents.

It was rewarding and at the same time, I would come home and thank God that all of my kids and grandkids were healthy. I enjoyed doing it. Every day was different. We never knew what was going to happen.

All of the sudden Mom perks up, "Oh yeah, I forgot to tell you this one other story, about Diane, who had Down Syndrome."

Her family was in the process of moving from one house to another. When we picked her up in the morning her mother said, "I'm running back and forth to the new house. So, grandma will be here when Diane gets home." We got to her house at the end of the school day. I didn't see anybody at the front door, but it was open. Diane got off of the bus and went inside. We got about a block down the road when Cindy said, "That didn't seem right." I agreed. We turned around and went back to her house. I got off of the bus and went inside calling, "Diane. Diane. Where are you?" I could hear her running from room to room, calling for her mom. You see, Grandma forgot and nobody was home. I brought her outside with me. Luckily a neighbor from across the street came and inquired if there was a problem. We told her what had happened. She offered to have Diane stay with her until her mom got home. That was quite the experience. After that, we made sure that there was an adult at home waiting for the kids when we dropped them off.

Oh, and part of my job was having to take CPR and First Aid, so that we would be able to act in an emergency. We were required to get re-certified every couple of years.

I comment, "It took a special person to do your job. Someone with a kind heart and a caring soul. I don't think that I could have done what you did."

Not too long ago, I was cleaning out some papers from school and found our reviews. Everything was marked, "excellent, excellent, excellent." And on the bottom my supervisor would write, "I am so happy to have Roula with our kids. We appreciate her so much. Blah, Blah, Blah..." Same thing with your dad. I found his papers, as well.

I had to eventually retire, to stay at home and care for your dad. The last year, I only worked the morning shift while your dad was still in bed. I was really lucky that Mr. Braham let me do that. I had a lot of sick time accumulated to use up before I retired. He knew my situation and because of all of my hard work and dedication over the years, he was always fair to me. Everything that I asked, he never refused me. I had a couple of really nice jobs that I really enjoyed. I worked at the school for a total of forty years when I finally retired in 2014.

Well, I think that's about all...

Holidays and Celebrations

HALLOWEEN

And the Winner for Best Costume Design Goes to...

We never had Halloween growing up in Cyprus. The picture that I showed you as a young girl with my classmates, where I was dressed up in a costume, was from a celebration we call Aprokria. It took place before the start of lent. I guess you can describe it as being similar to a Mardi Gras.

During Aprokria, the three weeks preceding lent, individuals of the Greek Orthodox faith indulge in carnival-type activities, including dressing up in costumes, parties, and the eating of meat. Roula is standing to the left of the girl with the "Stop/Go" shirt.

However, once I came to the United States and had kids, I started dressing you up for Halloween. Your costumes really started to become more elaborate once the three of you were in school and my mom, your YiaYia Athena, moved here from Cyprus and began living with us. I would come up with the ideas and your YiaYia would make the costumes. You know, we worked together. I'm trying to find more pictures besides the ones I gave you, but I'm having trouble finding them.

Anyways, I remember one year you were a Hawaiian hula girl and another year, a bride. You were also a mermaid and a pumpkin. Oh, and we made you into a three-layer cake. We cut and shaped cardboard and then dressed it up with material. The two layers were hung from your shoulders. The top layer you wore on your head, like a hat. You know, I had that costume up in the attic for years. Then I finally got rid of it.

Peter as half woman/half man, Irene as bride, Alki as Robin Hood

Oh, and the picture that I have of you during the church Halloween parade was of you dressed up like a native or a caveman. You were wearing a grass skirt and you had a bone in your hair at the top of your head. You were holding a spear and a shield.

I can't remember too many costumes for your brothers. Of course, there is the picture of your brother Pete as half woman/half man and Alki dressed up like Robin Hood. Mostly it was for you that we put our heads together for. The boys weren't as excited about dressing up. They were a little older, too, by the time your YiaYia came here to the United States. I do remember the time when Alki came up with the idea of wanting to be that guy from the rock band Kiss. So, I helped turn him into a cat.

Making your costumes was a fun project that your YiaYia Athena and I did together. We didn't want to dress you up in those ready-made costumes from the store. We wanted to be creative.

I recall, "Yes, I remember going to the church Halloween parties. Everyone had their cheap looking costumes on that they purchased from K-Mart. I would always win the prize for 'best costume' because..."

Mom interjects, "Because your costumes were original!"

THANKSGIVING TRADITIONS

Breaking the news to my boys, now ages 21 and 19, that we wouldn't be traveling to Youngtown to celebrate Thanksgiving this year with their YiaYia, Cousins, Aunts, and Uncles was nothing short of disappointing. You see, not only did our kids look forward to this annual celebration, my husband Brian referred to it as one of the best weekends of the year. Personally, I eagerly anticipated spending quality time with my family and close friends in my hometown. With the second wave of COVID-19 blanketing both Ohio and New York, my brothers each decided to stay home and celebrate with their immediate family. My Cousin Sue also made the decision to stay home, opting out of our homemade bread stuffing and settling for take-out this year. Although YiaYia was invited to both of my brother's homes, we took precautions and won the gift of having YiaYia at our house, here in Elma, this year for Thanksgiving. Trying to overcompensate by cooking and baking all of my boys' favorites, I quickly realized that I had cooked for sixteen to twenty people, as opposed to the eight that were actually going to eat.

It was the Friday after Thanksgiving, Mom and I were lazily sitting around, knowing that we had plenty of leftovers to get us through dinner, when we started reminiscing about the past. She asks, "Where do you want to start?" I asked her to recap again for me, her first experience celebrating Thanksgiving here in the United States. This is what she had to say...

We never celebrated Thanksgiving in Cyprus. When I first came to the United States, it was your Theia Lygia who prepared my first Thanksgiving turkey. You see, your Theia Eglie had just given birth on November 22 to your cousin Pete. She came home from the hospital on Thanksgiving Day that year, 1959. That is why Lygia brought the turkey over to Eglie and Paul's house. So we could celebrate together.

Our turkeys were never stuffed with a traditional bread stuffing. They would be stuffed with a mixture of rice and sautéed turkey gizzards and liver. Sometimes pine nuts and raisins would also be added to the rice stuffing. Actually, back in Cyprus, turkey with rice stuffing was traditionally served on Christmas. However, I don't remember eating turkey growing up. I'm not sure of the reason. Maybe we couldn't afford it. So, this was my first experience with Thanksgiving in the United States and eating turkey prepared this way.

After this first year, your Theia Eglie took over hosting Thanksgiving, because we would celebrate your cousin Peter's birthday in addition to the holiday.

I ponder for a moment, "What else would we have with the turkey and rice. I can't seem to remember?" Mom thinks, "No, that was it. We didn't have all of these side dishes like we do now. However, we always had pumpkin pie."

I ask, "What prompted you to take over hosting Thanksgiving?"

Well, our family was growing. Pete and Alki got married and started having kids of their own. There were too many people in our immediate family. I couldn't expect Eglie to have to cook for all of us. Plus, Peter K. moved away and we were no longer celebrating his birthday. So, that's when I took it over. It's been at least twenty-five years. And as the family grew, seating everybody became a challenge, as well as feeding everybody.

The grandkids had to sit in the laundry room to make room at the dining room table for the adults. At one point in time, we had ten adults plus the six boys.

I laugh at the reference to the laundry room, "Remember a couple of years ago when we tried to seat everybody in the living room/ dining room? The boys revolted. It wasn't Thanksgiving at YiaYia's house unless they sat in the laundry room for dinner."

Yes, Mom laughs. They were free to eat, drink (as they got older), laugh, and play cards down there without the adults meddling in their fun. A couple of years in a row, when the weather was nice, they even went outside and played football in the back yard. They would really have a lot of fun together on this day.

And each year we kept adding more food to the menu. As the boys got bigger, they had huge appetites. I think it was you that started making the bread stuffing.

I respond, "Yes, to this day, cousin Sue's favorite part of Thanksgiving is having 'real stuffing,' not the 'rice with the turkey liver,' that we grew up eating for so many years."

Of course, we would have mashed potatoes, Bobbie Ann always made the "make ahead" recipe from Taste of Home, with the cream cheese. Then we started adding sweet potatoes, sometimes baked or mashed. A couple of years in a row, we even had cheesy potatoes. Margie made those. There was cranberry sauce (out of the can), a vegetable, rolls with butter, mushroom gravy, and let's not forget about the 20-22-pound turkey. I would even bake a ham and slice some of it to put out on the buffet. Your Dad's favorite was the turkey wings. I always saved those for him. We had some really good-looking turkeys over the years. Some looked a whole lot better than they tasted. We made some mistakes over the years. There is definitely a skill to baking a perfectly moist turkey. But nobody minded.

The guys were always in a competition to see who could eat the most. Your brother, Pete, always won, with his plate stacked high with food. I think he always went back for seconds, too. I don't know where he managed to put all of that food in his 145-pound body!

Oh, and your family always loved to go Black Friday shopping the day after Thanksgiving. We had fun taking the boys to the Southern Park Mall and buying Dylan his birthday gift and letting them both choose their own Christmas presents from Pappou and I.

I reflect with a smile on my face, "I would always meet up with my girlfriends who were in Youngstown from out of town to celebrate Thanksgiving with their families. The girls would do a little boutique shopping during the day and then all of us, including the guys, would meet out at a restaurant for a nice dinner celebration in the evening. You and Dad would take care of the boys for us so that Brian and I could enjoy this day as well."

Yup, we did a lot of eating and a lot of shopping. That has been our Thanksgiving tradition.

I just remembered a funny story about when your father and I were visiting in Buffalo. Your boys were little and I think we were coming back from the park. We had such a nice time together when I said to them, "Maybe YiaYia and Pappou will move to Buffalo someday, so that we can be closer to you." Their response back to me, "But YiaYia, where are we going to go for Thanksgiving if you and Pappou move to Buffalo?"

And up until this year, except for maybe one other year, I think they have been celebrating Thanksgiving with me in Youngstown every year since they have been born.

VASILOPITA AND THE RINGING IN OF A NEW YEAR

No sooner had Christmas 2020 ended, that my son Tanner asked me, "Are you making vasilopita?" I immediately responded back, "Of course, I make it every year." He replies, "Oh no. You didn't make it last year." I ponder, "Hmmm, I didn't?" Both boys chime in, "NO YOU DID NOT!" I guess some traditions are hard to break. Especially those involving cake and a lucky coin...

It is January 1, 2021. I call Mom to wish her a Happy New Year and the first two questions out of her mouth are, "Did you cut your vasilopita? Who got the coin?" I reply, "Yes, I did and nobody found it yet. It must be in the second half of the cake. To everyone's disappointment, I guess we will all have to wait until tomorrow when I cut the rest." Mom responds, "Oh yes, that happens sometimes." We chat some more about how the vasilopita turned out and the highlights of our New Year's Eve celebrations. Then we conclude by making arrangements to talk the next day about Cypriot traditions and the Christmas season.

Let's start with Christmas. You know, growing up in Cyprus, Christmas was more of a religious holiday. But still not as important as Easter. We would go to church and that was about it. There wasn't a big celebration like here in the United States. Santa Clause never visited Cyprus. We didn't get presents or anything. However, I do remember having a Christmas tree in our home. We used to decorate it with different colored balloons. Nothing fancy.

As children, we would anxiously wait for the arrival of St. Basil on New Years. We would put our shoes out before going to bed on New Year's Eve. Then in the morning we would find some money and maybe some chocolate or candy in our shoes. Even then, we didn't get a lot. Your YiaYia Athena, my mom, couldn't afford too much. But it didn't matter to us. We were happy. And if we stayed up late enough on New Year's Eve, until midnight, we would cut our vasilopita. Whoever found the coin in the cake was guaranteed luck for the coming year.

The first of the year is St. Basil's name day. That is why there is a big celebration on this day. I pulled out my Cypriot cookbook and this is what it says,

> "The story behind St. Basil goes...
> 'When Caesarea was being attacked by the Cappadocians, St. Basil appealed to his people to help in the form of giving something of value. By a miracle the Cappadonians gave up their attack and St.

Basil, finding himself surrounded by valuables, baked some loaves in which he hid the precious objects.'

Everyone is happy on New Year's Day because Cypriots believe that they should behave in a way they wish to follow for the coming year" (Davies: 153).

In the United States, after the three of you were grown up and doing your own thing, your dad and I would go to your Theia Eglie and Uncle Paul's house on New Year's Eve. We would stay up until midnight, cut the vasilopita, and have a piece with a glass of champagne. According to the book,

"The first slice is given to the church, the second to the poor, the third is cut for the house and the rest of the cake is divided between the members of the family, starting with the most senior" (153).

We didn't do that in our house. We just cut it and ate it all ourselves. And another New Year's custom, which we never did in our family, but I've seen it on the Greek T.V. channel, is to break apart a pomegranate and spread the seeds at your front door. It signifies "good luck" for the coming year. You know, when I was in Cyprus, my cousin Androulla gave me this little gold pomegranate charm. I think I still have it somewhere. I'm going to look for it and show it to you next time you come home.

Mom pauses for a moment, "Let me think about what else we did during the holiday season... Do you want me to continue into the Theophany? It is something that the Greek Orthodox celebrate on the 6th of January. It is the Epiphany or baptism of Christ." I respond back, "Yes, I would love to hear about this celebration."

I couldn't wait for this day. I can close my eyes and still remember it so well... After the church service, the entire congregation would walk in a procession from Ayios Lazaros church to the Finikoudes by the sea. There was music and celebration. Just like we were in a parade.

We would end up on the fishing pier. The priest would say a few words as part of the service for the Epiphany. Then he would throw a cross into the sea. Immediately following, the priest would release two white doves, signifying the holy ghost. Then all of the young men would dive into the water off of the pier in an effort to retrieve the cross. The one who emerged holding the cross would have luck for the coming year.

There are some areas in the United States that do this ceremony. I think I've read about it occurring in New York City on the Hudson River and in Tarpon Springs, Florida. In fact, the priest from St. Johns Church, right here in Boardman, started doing this a few years ago. He goes to Mill Creek Park, in Youngstown. After the service, he throws the cross into Newport Lake. However, nobody jumps into the water to retrieve the cross. It's winter time and Newport Lake isn't very clean. The other local Greek Orthodox priests in the area started joining him in this celebration.

You know, we used to get this magazine called, "The Orthodox Observer." They used to show all of the celebrations that were occurring throughout the United States. We don't get it anymore. Maybe it's on Facebook now or what do you call it...the internet?

When congregations celebrate the Epiphany and stay in church, the priest performs the service and blesses water that is placed in a Baptismal font. The blessed water is then poured into small bottles and given to the parishioners. This water is used to bless their own homes. Sometimes the priest will even make a visit to the parishioner's homes in the new year and do the blessing with the holy water. And this signified the end of our Holiday celebrations...

After lunch on January 2, both Dylan and Tanner were "chomping at the bit" for me to cut the remainder of the vasilopita. The first reason was because they were ready for dessert. The second and most important reason was, they couldn't wait any longer to see who would pick the piece with the lucky coin in it. Their brotherly competition has yet to diminish over the years. I was even stumped. Normally, when I cut the cake, I can feel the coin when the knife cuts into it. So, it was a surprise to us all, as we waited for all four pieces to be served, turning them over one at a time to inspect the bottom, in hopes of catching a glimpse of the silver aluminum that was wrapped around the coin. Who was the lucky winner for 2021? Tanner, of course!

Recipe: Vasilopita– New Year's Cake

Ingredients:

3 cups flour

¾ stick of butter (6 Tbs.)

4 Tbs. vegetable, sunflower, or nut oil

1 cup sugar

5 oz. orange juice

2 Tbs. brandy

2 tsp. baking powder

1 Tbs. grated orange rind

4 eggs

1. In a large bowl, beat butter until soft, then beat in egg yolks, sugar, oil, and orange rind.
2. Gradually add the brandy and orange juice.
3. Lastly, fold in flour, baking powder, and whisked egg white.
4. Pour into a lined and buttered 9-inch springform pan.
5. Don't forget to sink a well washed coin that is wrapped in foil into the cake.
6. Decorate the top with slivered almonds (optional).
7. Bake in a preheated 350-degree oven for approximately 45 minutes until top is golden or until toothpick inserted in middle comes out clean.

NOT YOUR AVERAGE EASTER EGG HUNT

I'd be hard pressed to find another American family hovering around their kitchen table trying to catch in their mouth a slippery, slobbery hard-boiled egg, that is attached to a string and suspended from a light fixture. And did I mention, no hands were allowed?

Well, I guess you've figured out by now that we were not your average American family. Despite how hard we tried to acclimate to

American traditions, our Cypriot culture made some customs hard to part with, especially during Lent and the Easter holiday. Furthermore, with the lack of access to computers and Google for all of my childhood, I often had no explanation as to why we often celebrated Easter on a different Sunday than my fellow classmates. Whenever I asked an adult in my family, all I ever got was this response, "It has something to do with the calendar."

However, if you desire a more comprehensive explanation, I offer up the simplest version that I could find. According to Christianity. com, "The different date for Orthodox Easter comes from following the Julian calendar (implemented by Julius Cesar in 325 AD) that differs from the Gregorian calendar (implemented by Pope Gregory XIII in 1582) which is used by most western countries and Christian denominations. Consequently, the Orthodox Easter often occurs at a later date, on the first Sunday after the first full moon after the Spring equinox. The primary goal of creating the Gregorian calendar was to alter the time of Easter. Because Julius Caesar miscalculated the length of the solar year by 11 minutes, Pope Gregory XIII, felt that the Julian calendar had fallen out of sync with the seasons and further away from the spring equinox with each passing year."

Still confused? I encourage you to use the old standard that I have been using for most of my life, "It has something to do with the calendar."

CARNIVAL

Let's get back to that egg game. While it is customary for those who follow the Greek Orthodox faith to partake in various celebrations (referred to as Carnival) that involve fun and feasting, for the ten days preceding the start of Lent, the Sunday before lent was often our time to gather as a family and participate in this tradition. Although the specific details are somewhat vague, this is what my cousin Sue had to say, "Theia Lygia was masterful in how she tied *the egg to the string and then suspended it from the light fixture so that it swung, like a pendulum, from mouth to mouth. Afterwards, when the game was over, she would burn the string.*

Mom continues on...

LENT

Devout Cypriots, like my YiaYia Mariannou, my mother, and my Theia Eleni, would fast during lent for forty days preceding Easter. During this time, nothing derived from an animal, fish, or fowl is eaten. Although we didn't eat much meat growing up in Cyprus anyways, the kids would fast on certain days. The first day of lent was one of those days. As a family, we would go on a picnic. My mother would get bread from the local baker and with it we would have fruit, vegetables, olives, and wine. Although, I'm not sure how much of that wine I was drinking as a kid? The remainder of lent, I think we would fast on most Wednesdays and Fridays, in addition to the three days prior to receiving communion during holy week.

During Holy Week, the week preceding Easter, there are daily church services. On Good Friday, the ladies from the church go in early in the morning to decorate the Epitaphio (representing the tomb of Christ) with flowers. There is a special service on Friday afternoon where Christ is taken off of the cross and buried in the Epitaphio or tomb. Back in Cyprus, all of the priests and parishioners from four or five churches, would walk to the Acropolis with their Epitaphio. The remainder of the Good Friday service would be held there in the center of town with all the people.

Finally, we attend midnight mass on Saturday night into early Sunday morning. At midnight, the lights in the church go out. There is one oil candle at the holy altar. The priest takes this light and proceeds to light some of the candles that are being held by the parishioners attending mass. Each person then shares their light with others who are standing near them. When all candles are lit, the priest begins to sing "Christos Anesti," (Christ is Risen) an Easter hymn that celebrates Christ's resurrection. Soon we all join in with the song. Back in Cyprus, we would go outside at this point during the service and walk around the church. The priest would say The Gospel. Then the church doors would open. The lights would be back on. We would go inside for the remainder of the service.

> *Mom thinks for a moment, "There was a time when we used to bring that light home and light a special candle in our house. I'm not sure if anyone does that anymore?" I interrupt her thought, "All I remember is being really, really tired and the only thing keeping me awake was to play with the melting wax that was dripping down into the dixie cup that was around each candle." Mom laughs, "I know, we'd always come home with wax all over our hands and clothes. It was a mess." Mom laughs even harder thinking about the candles, "This one kid who was standing behind your Theia Eglie almost caught her hair on fire. I think he singed it a bit."*

EASTER SUNDAY CELEBRATIONS

We would finally get home from church around 2:00 a.m. It was then that our week-long celebration would begin. We would have our avgolemono soup, which I already mentioned in another story, and if we were up to it, begin the cracking of our Easter eggs. Traditionally died red, representing the blood and sacrifice of Christ on the cross, everyone gathers around the table, chooses their egg, and taps their egg against their opponent's egg saying "Christos Anesti" (Christ is Risen). The cracking represents Christ's resurrection. The individual whose egg does not crack continues on, playing his egg against other opponents.

Back in Cyprus, the kids who would win, would take their opponents' eggs. Here, we just eat the cracked eggs with our soup or for breakfast the next morning, along with our toasted easter bread and haloumi cheese. Sometimes we even continue the game with family as they come to the house for dinner. Oh, and we always died our eggs different colors to incorporate some American customs into our Easter celebration.

Finally, preparation for dinner would commence. We always serve pastichio, potato salad, stuffed grape leaves, and lamb. Many years ago, when you were very little, we would get our lamb directly from our friend, George Kyprianou, who raised lambs on his farm. He would butcher them for us and we would purchase half a lamb from him during the Easter season. None of it ever went to waste. Your father ate the liver and your Pappou Petros even ate the head.

I get lost in my thoughts for a moment...I cringe at the sight, embedded in my memory forever, of a lamb head on a sheet pan, roasting in the oven. It would take years before I was able to eat lamb again. In fact, I'm surprised that this did not turn me immediately into a vegetarian.

Once George quit raising lambs and sold his farm, we would source out lamb chops from local grocers. Your father would put them on the BBQ and the whole neighborhood would smell amazing. This tradition continues to this day.

As I mentioned, we would celebrate for an entire week. Another tradition was to make "flaounes," Easter cheesecakes. Flaounes are made using the same dough that we use to make Easter bread. We roll out individual squares that are then filled with a mixture of haloumi cheese, raisins, eggs, and mint. They are then brushed with an egg wash and sprinkled with sesame seeds before baking.

Mom thinks for a moment, "Back in Cyprus, we would have another picnic, the Friday after Easter. We would go to this little church where we would indulge in flaounes and hard-boiled eggs. I wonder if the church still exists..."

NFL Football with a Cypriot Twist

When you are raised by parents who grew up on an island in the middle of the Mediterranean Sea, watching football never topped the list of weekend activities. While my brothers, as adults, have found great joy in watching the sport, my lack of interest is evident by my glass-eyed stare and lack of enthusiasm whenever I have been forced to watch a football game on TV or attend one live and in person. However, this year was a bit different. The Buffalo Bills were playing against the Indianapolis Colts in a playoff game that had been in the making for twenty-five years. Brian and Tanner had "won the lottery" and had gotten tickets to attend the game on January 9, 2021. I opted to travel home to Youngstown to see my mom, promising to watch the game on TV at 1:00 p.m. Having gotten a little sidetracked in the morning, enjoying coffee and a walk thru Boardman Park with my friends, Gina (who had driven in from Michigan) and Cindy (a true Y-town girl, who never moved away), I hurried into the house a few minutes after kick-off. Mom had the game on the television.

She announced, "Oh you missed it. The one guy from the Bills 'attacked' the quarterback!"

With the plan to make Avgolemono soup for dinner, Mom and I sit down together to watch the rest of the game. For the first time, our excitement was epic, as the Buffalo Bills squeezed out a win over the Colts, with a score of 27-24.

Following the game, we head into the kitchen to put the finishing touches on our nourishing avgo (egg) lemono (lemon) soup. Mom proceeds...

After you boil your chicken, remove it from the stock pot and place it into a smaller pot. Growing up, we used whole chickens, but today I'm using chicken thighs. I then strain the broth into a large glass bowl, wash the pot, and return the broth back into the clean stock pot. Then, add a couple ladles of the strained stock to the chicken, for reheating later when it's time to eat. Now I bring the stock back to a boil and add one cup of rice. Let this simmer for about 20-30 minutes. You want the rice to be soft. Once the rice is cooked, we continue.

Side note...I have never known my mom to use anything but "Uncle Ben's Original Long Grain White Rice," in the orange box.

Using a hand mixer, beat 2 eggs in a bowl. You want to mix them really good. Then slowly pour in some lemon juice. I'm not going to measure it. Just pour it in. Maybe one-third of a cup? Then beat again until light yellow and fluffy. Then you add a little bit of water and beat some more.

I ask, "How much water?" Mom replies, "Just a little bit."

Then to the egg mixture, you begin to slowly ladle scoops of broth, stirring after each scoop. You do this a little at a time because you don't want the eggs to cook. Do it until the egg mixture becomes the temperature of the broth. It's called "tempering." Then you slowly add the egg mixture into the pot of broth, one scoop at a time, stirring after each scoop.

Mom comments to me, "See how it's thickening up?"

Now turn up the heat a little just until it is hot. You don't want to bring it to a boil. Then taste it to see if it needs more lemon or salt. But you can always add more in your bowl once it is served. Some people don't like it too salty or lemony.

Mom tastes it, "I think it's good."

Ladle the soup into a bowl and sprinkle it with cinnamon to taste. We always eat our boiled chicken on the side, sprinkled with salt and lemon juice. I suppose you can cut up the chicken and put it right in the soup. I think the Greeks do that. But this is my story. So, I'll tell it my way.

Mom concludes, "And that's about it. This is avgolemono soup."
As we sit down to eat, I ask, "Tell me some more about the traditions and customs associated with avgolemono.

People who are very religious, will fast for forty days before Easter. Following a predominantly vegan diet, except for fish, avgolemono soup is traditionally the first thing eaten, following midnight mass, to break the fast. It is comforting and light to the digestive system and is a way for individuals who have been fasting, to ease their way back into eating heavier meals, such as lamb, that is served on Easter Sunday. When your Pappou Petros came to live with us from Australia, I used to make it for him on Easter, sometimes waiting up until 2:30 a.m. This is the time he would get home from church after cantoring at midnight mass. We would make it for Christmas, too. Really, it was eaten all the time.

Soup was a staple growing up in Cyprus. If we were sick, my mom always made avgolemono for us. It has lots of health benefits; the chicken stock, rice, and lemon juice. And as I mentioned, it was very comforting. However, we didn't have all of this sickness growing up in Cyprus like we do now.

After living in the United States, we would travel back to Cyprus to visit. My sister Goulla, always had avgolemono soup for us to eat on the day of our arrival, before settling down to rest. In fact, a few years ago, my brother Marios drove in from Springfield, Ohio, to visit us here in Boardman. I thought he would like some soup on the day of his arrival. So, I made him avgolemono. He laughed and said, "Because I travelled, you made me soup. Just like my other sister!"

Mom pauses, "I don't know, Irene? I think I made it last year for you, when you came here for my knee replacement surgery." I reply back, "I can't remember. But it sure is good."

You know, in Cyprus, we would boil a whole chicken that we raised in our own backyard. Everybody had chickens. We picked eggs every morning. And if we needed a chicken for soup or to roast in the oven with potatoes, my mother would kill it and prepare it. We always had plenty of chicken. Other than that, we didn't eat a lot of meat. Maybe once a week, on Sunday or for holidays. On those days my mom would prepare a roasted chicken, keftedes (fried meatballs), vegetables like peppers and zucchini stuffed with ground pork and rice (I think to myself, commonly referred to by my cousins and brothers, as "stuffed stuff"), or a pork or lamb roast with green beans and tomatoes.

Mom pauses, "Do you know? Growing up, I never liked green beans. I was always forced to eat them when I was a kid. But now I love them."

And we didn't have ovens in our homes. My mom had to prepare our dish for the oven, then send it to the neighborhood bakery to be cooked. Sometimes we would drop it off in the morning on our way to church. Then we would stop and pick it up when it was done on our way home.

Oh, this is a funny story...One day, my mother paid a kid from the neighborhood to go to the bakery and pick up our meal. Well, on his way back to our house, he must have dropped it! He put it back in the pan the best way that he could, and brought it to our house, pretending that nothing happened. But your YiaYia Athena could tell that it didn't look quite right. I can't remember what we ended up eating that day. But it wasn't the roast that kid had brought home to us!

And talk about cholesterol! Maybe this was the start of my problem? I don't remember having real butter growing up in Cyprus. We used to put lard and sugar on our toast. My mother used to make her own lard. We would go to the butcher and buy the fat. I remember sitting down at the table and cutting it into little cubes. I always liked to help your YiaYia Athena in the kitchen.

My mother would then put the cubes in a big pot and render them down. She would freeze the fat (lard) that was to be used for cooking and on our toast. Then she would take the crispy cracklings that were left (similar to bacon) and make a sweet bread with them.

I remember years later, when your Theia Eglie went back to Cyprus to visit. Her sister, your Theia Ellou, was using lard to make cookies. Well, needless to say, Eglie was a little freaked out by that. I'm sure they were delicious.

I'm still kicking. It couldn't have been that bad!

We had no food waste back then. In fact, when your Pappou lived here with us, he ate up everything that the rest of us didn't want.

I always enjoyed going to the open market to shop with my mother and YiaYia. It was pleasant. You could go to the butcher and see whole lambs and pigs hanging. We would tell the butcher what parts we wanted and he would cut it fresh for us. If you wanted ground pork, he would grind it right there. Our meatloaf was called "rollo." I don't recall seeing any cows or eating any beef.

And of course, your father's mom and dad raised their own rabbits. They would kill and prepare those to eat. Rabbit is good.

Mom asks, "Do you remember when your dad would go hunting and bring rabbits home?" I cringe and reply back, "Oh, I remember!"

We ate a lot of beans and vegetables. My mother would make lentils with rice and caramelized onions, fava beans with swiss chard, and black-eyed peas with zucchini. We never complained. We ate whatever was put in front of us. We had plenty of eggs for breakfast, with haloumi cheese, toast, and jelly. We never ate cereal. With the neighborhood bakeries so close, we would go there to get special treats, like round koulouri (similar to a bagel) and homemade breads.

I reflect momentarily on the podcast that I was listening to on my drive to Youngstown the previous day. I say to mom, "I was just listening to a 'health expert' on my way here. He was saying that the best way to eat is according to your culture and the way that your ancestors ate.

For me, that would be the Mediterranean diet, that you are describing."

Mom follows up, "I like it when you come home. I get to cook good things we both like to eat."

Beach Vacations

Alki, Irene, Demos, and Peter on one of many beach vacations.

Because your dad and I grew up in Cyprus, we both loved to swim in the sea. However, when we moved to the United States, we lived in Youngstown. We weren't near any sandy beaches or ocean water, only lakes. When we had a family, we always took off in the summer and headed on vacation to places where there was an ocean. Over the years, we travelled to different cities in Florida, Virginia Beach, and Myrtle Beach. Later in life, your dad and I even went to Ocean City, Maryland, a couple of times.

Vacationing in the summer months was easy for us. Your father had worked at the steel mill for many years. He accumulated a lot of vacation time that he often took in the summer. I worked at the school in the cafeteria and had summers off, along with the three of you. So, we were never in any rush when we went on vacation. If we were driving, we'd go to AAA, get our Triptik and various maps, pack our car, and take off. Your dad would drive and I would navigate according to the Triptik. We had no phones or GPS. And we would travel in old cars, all crowded in with no air-conditioning. You kids would get cranky and start fighting. You would always end up crying because your brothers would pick on you. And your father and I just had to put up with the three of you for many hours in the car. However, we also travelled by bus to St. Petersburg, Florida, and even took the train once to Miami Beach when you were really little.

We rarely made reservations at a hotel/motel. Once we arrived at our destination, we would drive around and look for "vacancy" signs. Stop and ask to see a room. If it was clean, we would book it. I preferred a room with a small kitchen so that I could prepare meals. Although we went out to eat once in a while, it was unaffordable to dine out for every meal. Nothing fancy was needed because we spent most of our time on the beach.

Boardwalk photo of Roula and Demos.

HOLLYWOOD BEACH

Your Theia Lygia and cousin George often came with us when we went on vacation. One year we decided to take the train to Miami, Florida. From Youngstown, the train took us first to Washington, DC. We had a little layover. Because we were in the main area, I can't remember what it was called, we decided to take a walk. I remember seeing the White House.

Mom Pauses, "You were very little. Do you remember this trip?" I respond, "No, I don't remember anything about this trip."

Then the train continued on to Hollywood Beach. It was near Miami. We found a place to stay on the beach. It was there that we met a Greek girl. I can't remember her name. But she took us places, including the zoo. I have to look through my pictures. I think I have a picture of her holding you at the zoo. We met nice people every place that we went. And it was fun on the train. I remember your brothers and George running back and forth, up and down the aisle.

I asked my cousin George to reflect on this trip. He too, was quite young and can't remember a lot. However, this was his response...

"I don't recall being in Miami or Hollywood Beach with you guys. Unless maybe it was the time when I got bongos as a souvenir and was playing them all the time and driving everyone crazy? I'm pretty sure there is a picture of me playing bongos on the motel balcony. There must be other photos from that trip as well that would show us all together."

VIRGINIA BEACH, VIRGINIA

Your cousin George turned 16 in December of 1970. He had just received his driver's license when his father, your Uncle Christ, bought him a new car. In the summer of 1971, your cousin George and Theia Lygia invited us to drive to Virginia Beach with them. I don't know what I was thinking, letting a 16-year-old drive our family all the way to Virginia Beach. But I don't remember being scared. We all jumped into his car. There were seven of us altogether. Your dad sat in the front with George and coached him on his driving, while the rest of us crammed in the back seat.

When we finally arrived, we drove around until we found a place to stay. During our stay, we met a Greek family from Canada. They had a young daughter that George became friendly with. If I'm not mistaken, he kept in touch with her for many years following the trip.

Once again, I reach out to George and ask him about our adventure to Virginia Beach...

"That was the trip where we smelled fish cooking every day and Demos (your father) said, 'It must be the Greek people in the apartment across the hall from us.' Yes, it was the Nifakis family from Montreal. The girl's name is Debbie (actually Despina). She was in Phoenix a couple of years ago for a convention. We met for dinner."

Although I was just shy of five years old, I have one memory of this trip. It is of my Theia Lygia asking all of us to roll down the car windows as we approached our destination, encouraging us to, "Smell the sea air."

ST. PETERSBURG, FLORIDA

The summer we went to St. Petersburg started off with Betsy and Marios visiting us here in Boardman. They wanted to take you back to Cincinnati with them for a short visit. After a few days or a week, I can't remember exactly how long you were there, we drove to Cincinnati and picked you up. Marios took us to the bus station in Cincinnati where we got on a bus that took us to St. Petersburg, FL.

I think for a few moments, "I remember being in St. Petersburg. However, I don't remember staying with Uncle Marios and Aunt Betsy. Nor do I remember taking the bus all the way to Florida and back. I must have blocked that part out of my memory."

Mom adds, "I know for sure that you were not happy staying with your Aunt and Uncle alone without the rest of your family being there."

It was many, many hours on the bus to St. Petersburg. That was one of the few times that I actually made a reservation. It was a hotel/motel called, "Treasure Island." The room that they first gave us wasn't very good. I remember it smelling really bad and it was located way in the back. However, we got there very late and we were all exhausted. We had no choice but to stay there for one night. The next morning, I went to the office and expressed my disappointment and told them that we would be leaving. The manager was apologetic and encouraged us to stay by placing us in a different room. We ended up moving to a really nice suite with a kitchen and living room area where we could all spread out and be comfortable.

I interject, "Yes, I remember now. When we were moving out of the first room, you told me to look under the beds in case anything rolled under there during our very short stay. I spotted something and reached for it. To my surprise, it was a ring!" Mom interrupts, "I still have that ring!" Surprised, I say "You do? Well, my brothers were a little jealous that I had found a treasure under the bed at the Treasure Island Motel. When we got to the new room, either Pete or Alki, I can't remember which brother, looked under the bed, spotted something and announced, 'Whatever it is, it's mine, it's mine!' To his dismay, it was a dead cockroach!"

And then of course, because we took the bus, we didn't have a car. We would walk everywhere, including the beach and even the grocery store. We'd have to carry all of our bags from the store back to our room at the hotel. But then, we met a family from Toronto. They had a son around your brothers' ages. For the rest of our trip, they offered to take us places, including the grocery store. They were nice and a really big help.

St. Augustine, Florida

Peter, Roula, Irene, and Alki in Daytona Beach, Florida.

Now this was a fun trip. We finally got to St. Augustine and we were trying to look for a hotel. Nothing was available in town or along the beaches of St. Augustine, so we continued driving along the coast. It was about halfway in between St. Augustine and Daytona Beach, when we saw a new condo development with a "For Rent" sign posted out front. We stopped in the office and inquired about a place to stay. Boy it was brand new, beautiful, right on the beach, and secluded. Kind of in the middle of nowhere. At first, we rented for one week. But we liked it so much, we decided to stay for another week. I remember for sure that we paid only $250 per week to stay in a brand-new condo. And of course, your dad had a lot of vacation time because he had been working at the steel mill for so many years. There was no hurry for us to get back, especially because it was summer and you were all off from school.

This was the year we decided to go to Walt Disney World. We got up real early in the morning and drove there, with plans to enter the park as soon as it opened and stay the entire day. We were one of the first cars to arrive, early that morning. We parked and enthusiastically entered The Magic Kingdom.

Mom pauses and asks me, "Do you remember Space Mountain?"
I cringe, "Oh yes, I remember. You all tricked me and made me go on
it. I was terrified!"

I was tricked going on Space Mountain. I had no idea what it was all about. We stood in line and as we got closer, I read the sign that said, "If you have a heart condition or are pregnant, you may exit here." That's when it hit me. This might not be the ride for me. But I hesitantly got on. You sat with your dad and I was with the boys. I was so scared. I couldn't believe that I had gotten on a roller coaster! When I got off, I said, "Oh my gosh. Never again!" You were afraid as well. But your brothers...they wanted to get back in line and ride. After spending the whole day at Walt Disney World, we decided it was time to leave.

We walked out to a sea of cars, having no idea where ours was parked. We didn't think about remembering where we parked when we first arrived. Nobody told us that we needed to remember the Disney character section that we were parked in. And to top it off, it started to rain! I thought to myself, "Oh boy are we in trouble." Adding to the stress were your brothers, who were running around the parking lot trying to look for our car. I thought that I was going to lose them, too. At first, I suggested that we all go back inside the park and wait until closing. This way, cars would start to leave, the parking lot would thin out, and we'd be able to find our car. Finally, this lady approached us on a golf cart. She was a park employee. I explained to her that we were having trouble finding our car. She asked me what time we had arrived. I told her 9:00 a.m. She knew the exact location where cars were being parked at that time. She invited us to jump onto her golf cart and she took us right to our car. As we were driving through the parking lot, I started noticing that the parking lot was sectioned off by Disney characters.

After that, I learned my lesson. Every time we went somewhere with a lot of cars, I always made a mental note of where we were parked.

MYRTLE BEACH, SOUTH CAROLINA

I think it was the first time we went to Myrtle Beach...

We got there and it was very late. Everybody was tired and we needed to find a place to sleep. We booked the first place we found. But only for one night, so that we could get some rest. It was a real dump. The next morning, we walked up and down until we found a better place to stay that was on the beach. We packed up and moved.

Mom asks, "Can you imagine doing that with three kids? Brian would go crazy." I reply back, "I agree. Brian would not be up for that."

By the time we finally got settled in our second motel, your dad was so anxious to swim. He put his bathing suit on and dove right into the ocean. The minute he did that, he got stung by a jelly fish! However, people on the beach advised us on what to do for a jelly fish sting and we were able to take care of it right away.

VIRGINIA BEACH, VIRGINIA

Some years we would go back to some of the places that were closer, like Virginia Beach. This second time around, the weather was so lousy. It wouldn't stop raining. Your father and I were stuck in a motel room with three kids. We didn't know what to do with you.

Thinking about this trip for a moment, I have a vague recollection. I interrupt mom, "If I'm not mistaken, this was the year the movie Jaws was released? It must have been the summer of 1975. Dad took the three of us to the theatre while we were in Virginia Beach. After seeing Jaws, I was terrified to go back in the ocean." Mom doesn't recall this but continues on...

This was the time that your brother Alki, bought a hermit crab. He had it next to his bed when we he went to sleep. However, when he woke up in the morning, he realized that the crab had escaped from its little cage. We ended up finding it in Alki's bed!

We had plans to stay in Virginia Beach for a week. But after several days of nonstop rain, we made the decision to leave. We didn't want to waste the rest of our vacation by going home. I called your Uncle Marios and we made the decision to drive to Cincinnati to stay with him and Betsy for a few days. Unknowingly, it was a really long drive. I'm not even sure how your dad and I figured out how to get to Cincinnati from Virginia Beach. But we eventually got there. Your dad loved to drive. I never helped him with the driving because I wasn't comfortable driving on freeways and in areas that I was not familiar with. I still don't drive out of town.

FORT LAUDERDALE, FLORIDA

We ended up in Fort Lauderdale one summer because Betsy's family offered us their condo to stay in. We thought it was a good idea at the time. But boy was that a big mistake. Besides me worrying about us breaking or ruining anything, that was the year I let your brother Pete bring his girlfriend, MaryAnne. So, I had to keep my eye on them, too. I was on edge all week and had to clean the entire condo myself before we left. So actually, this was not a good vacation for me. I did way more work than I had anticipated. From then on, I opted for a hotel room.

Mom pauses, "We had a lot of fun adventures!"

CYPRIOT PRIDE: NIAGARA FALLS, ONTARIO CANADA

We had two cars full, following one another. The first car George drove with the cousins; Peter, Alki, and you (Irene). The second car your father drove, with the adults: Theio Christ, Theia Lygia, and me (Roula). When we arrived in Niagara Falls, one of the first things that we did was go to the Wax Museum. Well, your Uncle Christ approached the ticket counter and started talking to the lady standing behind it. She wasn't responding to him, so he started yelling at her. Little did he know, that she was a wax figure! When we finally got inside, he started talking to a former President, I can't remember which one. However also, a wax figure. He thought the president was real. It was so funny.

I reflect on this trip as well. "I remember being in the motel room where George was staying with his mom and dad. Theio Christ had fallen asleep on one of the beds. These beds were also "massage beds." All you had to do was insert a quarter. Cousin George put a quarter in as a joke on his father, who woke up instantly and started yelling. We thought it was funny. Theio Christ, not so much." Mom laughs and continues...

On the way back, crossing the border into the United States, the customs officers ask you, "Where are you from?" We coached everybody to say, "The United States." The first car with you kids in it went through, no problem. George pulled forward and was waiting for us. When it was our turn, the customs officer asked us, 'Where are you from?" We all took our turns saying, "The United States." However, when they got to Uncle Christ, he proudly announced, "Cyprus!" We all thought to ourselves, "OH SHOOT!" We had our passports, but they were in the trunk of our car. The officer told us to pull over. We had to get out to retrieve our passports, show them to the officer and answer a bunch of questions. They finally let us cross into the United States.

Mom announces, "That was an inconvenience!"

Conclusion

JUST GO FOR IT

Little did we know that some minor inconveniences along the way would be worth their weight in gold. It was a trip over three years in the making. Our family excursion to Cyprus was finally going to happen. Despite some minor set-backs that caused us to cancel in 2020, such as a world-wide pandemic, we were ready to go on May 22, 2023. Nothing was going to hold us back this time. I knew that it was now or never. Everything aligned perfectly. The five of us, YiaYia (Roula), my husband Brian, my sons Dylan and Tanner, and myself, committed to this adventure. In addition, my two cousins, Peter and Sue Kalochoritis, decided to join us, making this a true family reunion.

Roula takes us on a walking tour of the Finikoudes.

From the time we left our house in Elma, New York, drove to Toronto, flew to London's Heathrow Airport, and flew to Larnaca, Cyprus, we arrived approximately 24 hours later. Despite feeling and looking as though we had been through a war, we were greeted at the airport by several family members who were eager for our arrival and assisted in getting all of us and our luggage to The Golden Bay Hotel. This would be our Cypriot home for the next two weeks.

It didn't take long for us to realize that having YiaYia (Roula) here with us would be nothing but an asset. Upon first impression, the locals considered us to be annoying tourists. However, once YiaYia began to work her magic, conversing with them in their native Greek Cypriot language, we became their people. The hospitality shown to us throughout the Island was exemplary. The locals were smitten by Roula's charm and the reason for her trip. After all, it had been seventeen years since she last stepped foot onto her Island of birth. Much too long in the eyes of her family and friends, who missed her dearly. Much too long in the eyes of the locals she befriended this time along the way.

Mehmet Ali is one of the first streets Roula remembers living on.

While here, Roula began to come into her own. If I had to describe it in one sentence, I would say this, "My mom turned into a young girl once again." The minor pains of aging and her daily life in the U.S, began to melt away as she walked about the island with an air of energy, confidence, and joy. On several occasions she commented, "My knees don't even hurt here in Cyprus." She led us through the streets where she grew up and reflected upon her life on the Island.

Walking on the Larnaca Pier at the Finikoudes, Roula told the story of coming here after getting her first pair of high-heeled shoes. The slats in the pier were wide, her heel got stuck, and scraped up as she tried to pull it out. Needless to say, as a young girl, she was quite upset. We all chuckled as we followed along with her on this journey through time. As we drove past the Larnaca jail, where Roula spent a few days as a young teen she pointed and said, "That's my jail!" Not wanting to hide or forget her past, but having vivid memories of the places where she had been.

I think we can all agree that although it was for only a short seventeen years that she lived here, Roula's experiences were vast and her roots grow deep on the Island of Cyprus. Like Aphrodite, the Goddess who emerged from the sea onto the Island, Roula also has been honored and admired for her beauty over the years. However, beauty is not her only asset. Roula, affectionately known as YiaYia by her family, exudes love, honesty, strength, and resilience.

On one of our last days in Cyprus, fatigued from all of the eating, visiting, and sightseeing, the seven of us set up on the beach for a day of rest and relaxation. The warm summer temps in Larnaca were just starting to arrive, making the Mediterranean Sea a bit chilly for most of us to enjoy. However, not for Roula, who jumped up out of her chair and announced that she was going to take a swim. We didn't pay much attention to her at the time. A few minutes later my cousin Sue and I glanced up to see my mom backstroking deeper and deeper into the water, her legs kicking and her arms methodically moving over her head. Eventually she stood up and started waving her hands, from us towards the water as she loudly shouted, "Come on! Just go for it!" We were left no choice but to accept her invitation, as we all got up from our chairs, entered the water, and joined in on the fun.

Roula reunited with her sister Goulla (left) and cousin Marianna (right).

Reflection

Saying goodbye to our Cypriot family was bittersweet. If my cousins, Maro and Niki, from my dad's side of the family, had it their way, they would keep their Theia Roula in Cyprus with them forever. In the lobby of our hotel, Roula's sister, Goulla, was in tears at the thought of never seeing us again. We posed for photos with family in an attempt to capture the special moments shared that we will have forever in our hearts. Until next time, as promises were made to call and FaceTime every opportunity we could.

Proyiayia Roula with Averie

These days, Roula spends most of her time reading, puttering around the house, and spending time with the ladies at church. They cook and bake in abundance for various events and fundraisers. YiaYia lives for her family, especially her first great-granddaughter, Averie. She puts her family first and enjoys cooking for them and spending as much time with them as she can. She takes the initiative to reach out to her grandchildren, her friends, and other family members, often inviting them over for a visit and always something to eat and drink. She's known for her never-ending bowl of cashews and cut up cheese, a glass of wine, a beer, or maybe even a shot of Metaxa or Ouzo. And there is always a sweet treat prepared, "just in case." Her grandsons all agree that YiaYia's scrambled eggs are unbeatable.

When the television is on, she is tuned into the Greek channels that she pays extra for as part of her Dish Network package. She watches the Greek and Cypriot news and looks forward to her Greek soap opera that airs nightly on the Antenna channel. You can find her recapping the drama with her sister Goulla on the telephone.

Roula is never afraid to voice her opinion. She gives her advice when asked (and even when not asked) and has an open mind and progressive view of the world. She gives of her time freely and when she's had enough, she sets her boundaries and lets others know. When she says "yes" it is a "yes" for her and when she says "no" it is a "yes" for her.

When I asked my mom to reflect back and describe her life these days, this is what she had to say...

Looking back on my journey, I sometimes wonder what my life would have been like if I never left my country. My recent trip to Cyprus brought me a lot of happy memories. It was a joy to share all of it with my family who traveled with me.

But fate brought me to this country and I have no regrets. I am very pleased with what I accomplished in my life. With my beautiful and loving family around me, my life is complete. I am so very proud of them and I love them so much. I hope they are proud of me and of their heritage and continue my legacy.

Mom stops and asks me, "Well, what do you think?" I am choked up and have tears in my eyes as I respond, "I think that is perfect."

Acknowledgments

To my husband Brian, thank you for welcoming YiaYia into our home and for loving her unconditionally for over thirty years. I know you enjoy our Cypriot "round tables." Just admit it.

My two sons, Dylan and Tanner, your computer skills are undeniable. I appreciate your patience as I translated these conversations into a computer document. Thank you for being a part of this journey with me. I hope you enjoy reading these stories through the eyes of your beloved YiaYia. As your mother, I have big shoes to fill.

I am blessed to have you as my brothers, Peter and Alki. Our lives growing up together have been nothing but joyful. I look forward to creating many more memories with you as we journey through life.

My cousins Sue and Peter, you accompanied your Theia Roula and my family on our epic "Big Fat Cypriot Vacation." I can't wait for our next adventure.

And to my cousin George, you volunteered your time meticulously editing the photos for this book. You've been an integral part of my parents lives since the beginning. For this I am grateful.

With gratitude to Rick's writing group. You encouraged me to start writing about my mom and gave me the motivation and guidance to follow-through to completion.

Deborah Sullivan, as one of Rick's writers, you put in the hours necessary to edit this book. Thank you for seeing the value in my work and for recognizing the greatness in my mother.

My father Demos Santamas, I am honored to have been your daughter. Although you are no longer here, your memory is eternal and your spirit lives on through me.

Family dinner on the Mediterranean Sea.
From left to right: Dylan, Brian, Tanner,
Irene, Roula

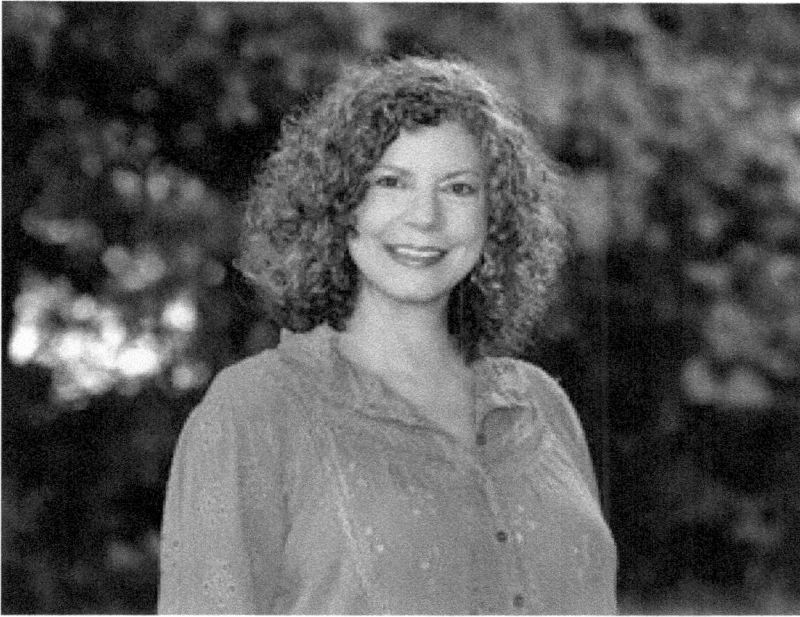

Growing up in Youngstown, Ohio, as a first generation Cypriot is the foundation in which Irene Santamas-Kulbacki models her way of being. Although she's lived in Buffalo, New York, for over thirty years, she still considers herself a Y-town girl at heart. She is deeply rooted in both her upbringing and culture, making it a mission to infuse them both into the lives of her sons and husband. Since moving away, Irene and her mom Roula speak daily, if not multiple times per day. Their relationship is tightly woven together, despite the 200 miles that separate them.

Irene has been a certified yoga instructor for the past twenty years and spends most days walking, reading, gathering with friends, and writing. She is a lifelong learner and is inspired by her connection to nature and her interactions with others. As the owner of Useful Gatherings, she is dedicated to bringing women together, in a retreat style format, who want to make positive changes in their lives and in the world.

www.ingramcontent.com/pod-product-compliance
Lightning Source LLC
Chambersburg PA
CBHW051716090426
42738CB00010B/1934